SAINT HONEY
and
OH DAVID, ARE YOU THERE ?

The two plays in this volume introduce another aspect of the talent Paul Ritchie has already confirmed with his novels THE PROTAGONIST and CONFESSIONS OF A PEOPLE LOVER.

SAINT HONEY is in fact a stage adaptation of THE PROTAGONIST, a highly successful novel for which Paul Ritchie was awarded an Arts Council Bursary. A man called Honey, at the end of his spiritual tether, arrives at the Listers' boarding house to rent a room where he can find the peace and oblivion he so desperately needs. But his withdrawn silence works like a catalyst on the frustrated desires and aggressions of the other members of the household - Alf Lister, the war veteran who lives off memories of his virility while nursing a game leg; Ted Ward, the ex-boxer, whose finest memory is of the day he fought 'the great Dempsey'; Moll, an aggressive, insensitive woman, whose knowledge of character is confined to what she has seen on the films, and who clings fiercely to the remnants of her sexual attractiveness; Hinds, the deaf Irishman with whom Honey is to share; and Dot Lister, who alone suspects that Honey, hysterically accused by the others of being variously a weakling, a madman and a homosexual, may in fact be a saint.

OH DAVID, ARE YOU THERE ?, the brilliant and complex one-acter which completes this volume, deals with the collapse of the illusions with which an old couple have attempted to bolster up the terrible failure of their lives.

Paul Ritchie was born in Sydney, Australia, and became a successful painter. In 1962 he turned to writing and had his first novel published by Cassell in the same year. He has since written two more novels, and is now completing a fourth. He is married, and lives on Ibiza.

OTHER C AND B PLAYSCRIPTS

* These plays are represented for dramatic presentation by
C & B Theatre, 18 Brewer Street, London W 1

PLAYSCRIPT 6

'saint honey' &
'oh david,
are you there?'

paul ritchie

CALDER AND BOYARS · LONDON

First published in Great Britain 1968
by Calder and Boyars Limited
18 Brewer Street, London W 1

Printed in Great Britain by
Latimer Trend & Co Ltd
Whitstable, Kent

SAINT HONEY

CONTENTS

CHARACTERS

ALF LISTER	:	A veteran of world war one.
DOT LISTER	:	Alf's wife. A faded woman in her early forties.
"SAINT" HONEY	:	A man in his early thirties.
TED WARD	:	A tall, gaunt man of seventy-three. A friend of the family.
MOLL EDWARDS	:	Dot's sister. A thin, dark woman of about forty.
HARRY HINDS	:	A man in his thirties.
ENID BARLOWE	:	A girl in her twenties.

ACT ONE

SCENE: A living room in a tenement house
in an industrial town: an ordinary room
furnished in an ordinary way: arm chairs,
sofa, table, sideboard, mantlepiece, bric-a-
brac. A section of the kitchen can be seen ‐
back wall approached by a rise. In the centre
of the left wall there is a door opening on to a
hall which leads to the upper regions of the
house.
TIME: After dinner on a spring evening. As
the curtain rises, ALF appears to be sleeping
in an armchair, one leg resting on a foot stool.
He is a bald, florid, heavily-built man in his
sixties. As he sleeps there is a background
of electronic music fading into the sounds of
war. ALF stirs and suddenly jerks awake.
Silence. He gets up and limps to the sideboard and opens it. Rummages inside.
Gestures frustratedly. Off stage a door slams.
ALF hurries back to his chair and immediately
feigns sleep. The hall door handle rattles.
DOT enters with HONEY. DOT is a middle-
aged woman rather worn and ill-kept but not
slovenly, not unattractive. She is dressed
simply in house clothes: her hands bare and
raw looking. Somewhere down the line there
was good breeding in this woman. HONEY
might be thirty or more. A pale, good-
looking man who, for all that, might be wearing a mask. He is dressed neatly though not
well in a dark suit and carries a suitcase.

DOT: Now put your bag down, Mr. Honey. Anywhere will
            do... that's right, by the door will do. Alf, are you
            awake? (silence) He's probably dozed off again.
            Alf? (She goes and shakes his shoulder) Alf dear,
            wake up. Mr. Honey.....

ALF: What.... what's that .... what?

DOT: Alf, I want you to meet Mr. Honey. He's come
            about the room - the share with Hinds.

ALF: (glancing at HONEY) I thought you might have been
            the Insurance man but no matter. The point is -
            are you Irish? (HONEY smiles and shakes his head)
            Well that's a blessing anyway. Hinds' pal, the other
            one, wore his blessed boots to bed as if this place

had been the Pope's best boarding house. But we
soon sent him packing, didn't we, Dot? (she nods)
Mind you, I've had to consider the fact that that Hinds
isn't much better.

DOT: (to HONEY) It's only because he has to wear gum
boots at the public laundry. And he's always washing
his socks.

ALF: He stinks.

DOT: Alf, don't say that. Mr. Honey's going to share.

ALF: It's true. Everytime he comes in here to give this
old leg o' mine a rub I have to turn away my face.

DOT: Alf, that's not true and you know it. Don't take any
notice of him, Mr. Honey - Alf likes his little joke.

ALF: That's right, that's right, deny me my opinion and
stick up for that good-for-nothing... it's always
been the same with you. (to HONEY) If she had her
way she'd fill this place with every stray and pervert
in creation. (DOT sighs and moves towards the
kitchen) Now where are you off to?

DOT: To warm up some tea. (she goes out)

ALF: (grunts) Anyway as I said... you'll see, see if I'm
telling the truth or not. The point is I won't have any
more Irish here. I'd rather have an Oriental than an
Irishman here. Anyway you don't look Irish. Dot,
Mrs. Lister that is, has a soft spot for them though I
can pick 'em a mile away. Now drat this leg o' mine.
Hole in it, you know. Look, sit down - she should
have asked you before but that's women all over -
tea if you mind! Any one will do... that's right
(HONEY sits opposite). Hole, you know, big as an
egg... just before the armistice. Blasted Hun
chucked a bomb into a hole where I was (he fiddles
with his belt) but look here, you just take a gander
for yourself and feel the steel in there. (he raises
his shirt and exposes a part of his hip) There, see
what I mean? Now you can see what I've had to put
up with all these years, see what I've suffered for
this bloody nation. Now go on, put your fingers in
the pit of it and feel the steel.

HONEY: If it's all the same to you...

ALF: Oh it won't hurt if that's what you're afraid of. I just want you to know what I've had to put up with all these years though there was a time when this leg o' mine was as good a leg as ever made. I played a lot of football one time. Now look, you going to touch it?

HONEY: I'd rather not if you don't mind.

ALF: (readjusting his dress) Well, it's grim enough I'll grant you that what with the Huns and the quacks having a go at it but in spite of them it simply refused to perish, now what do you think of that?

HONEY: I think you must have a very stubborn, a very remark-able leg.

ALF: Oh, it's more than that let me tell you. It's .. it's.. I'll tell you what it is. It gives me hell sometimes though Hinds comes down when it suits him mind you to give it a bit of a rub though his hands are rough even if it helps to get the circulation going so that I can hobble about a bit. I keep telling Dot that - Mrs. Lister - for her hands are dry and she's a bit squeamish on the job. Anyway, there you are seeing me crippled in the course of duty so they say if you believe that bunk which I don't and I ... one of the best... a right good centre half you know. Now you see me sitting here with this leg up, warming it up a bit, and me getting fatter all the time. It has some weight to carry, let me tell you. (pause) Some weight all right... some bloody weight.

       (DOT enters with two cups of tea - hands
       them around)

DOT: I put two sugars in each cup - I hope it's all right.

HONEY: Thank you. (sips) It's a fine cup of tea.

DOT: I just warmed it up.

ALF: It's tea, isn't it?

       (DOT nods and moves towards kitchen)

Now where are you going?

DOT: To top up the kettle in case you want some more.

ALF: (grunts)   Not for me.

           (As DOT goes out he turns confidentially to
           HONEY)

        The trouble is, tea makes you leak a bit and what with
this leg o' mine the way it is I don't want to be out
there all the time. Now look, if you go in with Hinds
your lot will be thirty bob plus light. Mind you, it
isn't much these days considering we could get more
if we wanted.

HONEY: (withdrawing his wallet)   I'll pay now.

           (He takes out two pound notes and offers them
           to ALF)

ALF: Mind you, we ought to speak with Hinds being only
fair though on the other hand I don't see why we
should, blowed if I do. Yes, you can pay now and I'll
fix it with Hinds. Eh, Dot, mister... mister....

HONEY: Honey.

ALF: Mr. Honey wants to pay.

           (He takes the money as DOT appears, a
           dishcloth in her hands)

DOT: But Alf, I've been thinking it over. Shouldn't we
first check with Hinds seeing he's been here such a
long time?

ALF: Now why should we have to check with Hinds. He
doesn't pay for a double now, does he? He's got
to take pot luck the same as the rest of us. What
do you say, Mr. Honey?

HONEY: If there's going to be any difficulty I could find somewhere else. After all, there's always an empty
room somewhere.

DOT: Oh there's rooms all right - pokey little boxes you
wouldn't put a dog in. You'd be all right here, you
know, wouldn't he, Alf?

ALF: Of course he would. Hinds and Honey in the big
double sounds a pretty respectable firm to me.
Now you go and get a ten bob note for the gentleman,
my girl, or I'll do it myself.

(Straining, he raises his buttocks only
to resettle as DOT gently restrains him)

DOT: Please, Alf, don't upset yourself - of course I will.

ALF: And bring me my medicine while you're at it.

(DOT goes out)

Well, that's that, Mr. Honey - worrying about what
Hinds will say. He can go jump in the lake for all I
care. Been here too long that's his trouble. If
they're here too long they get a false sense of owner-
ship and expect the privileges of the family and it's
always me who has to cope with them.

(DOT enters with the money and a glass of
port. She hands both to ALF who gives HONEY
his change as he drains the glass)

Good Lord, it's a bit off that port, you know.

DOT: But it couldn't be.

ALF: Now listen here, when I say port's off it's off.

(As he glares at her TED WARD peeps his
head around the hall door)

TED: Lo, everybody. How's the boy, Dottie?

DOT: Moll's up there with him now. He's all right, Ted,
thank goodness. The doctor said....

ALF: I don't want to hear, I don't want to hear what any
old vet had to say. Now you come in here and have
a drink, Ted.

TED: Thanks, Alf, but I won't bother. (He enters)

ALF: Oh yes you will.

(He gestures to DOT to go and bring a glass.
DOT sighs and goes out)

Now Ted, I want you to meet Mr. Honey - the new
share with Hinds.

HONEY: (standing) How do you do?

(TED shakes HONEY'S limp hand)

ALF: Now there, Mr. Honey, stands a man who was forty seven years in America.

TED: Ay.

ALF: Forty seven years, mind you, before he came back to the Old Dart. Now tell him Ted why don't you about that time in New Mexico when you had to clobber that bloke with a hammer after he'd done what he did with that kid - the filthy swine!

TED: I would, Alf, you know that but I'm a bit tired. I've been out as you know. Went down to Blackwater to see my sister Amy and for all the good it did I might as well not have gone. Not only is she as deaf as a post but she kept calling me Mr. Chambers.

ALF: Of all the.... (he bursts into a raucous chuckling)

TED: Now hold it, Alf.

ALF: Mr. Chambers my bleeding foot. I'll have you know, Mr. Honey that Ted Ward here fought Jack Dempsey - the greatest heavyweight the world has ever seen and yet there's his own flesh and blood calling him - Mr. Chambers.

TED: Go easy on her, Alf - remember she's an old lady. Besides, you ought to tell Mr. Honey that Dempsey knocked me out in the third round.

ALF: Ugh - with a lucky punch.

TED: Some say it was but then (he shakes his head) it was still a beauty.

(he addresses HONEY)

But after it was all over Dempsey came to me and said - Ted, he said, Ted me boy, you had me worried for a bit - just look at that mouse under me eye. It was there all right - as big as an apple. But he was a great champion Jack - a great guy.

ALF: He had a lucky punch - that's all.

TED: Well, it's all in the game, Alf.

ALF: Some people have all the luck while the rest of us have
         no luck at all - now blast this leg of mine!

         (TED pats him on the shoulder)

TED: Steady on, old soldier.

         (to HONEY)

         Alf show you the hole in his leg yet?

         (HONEY nods)

         What a terrible thing that was - just terrible.

ALF: Terrible he calls it.   I call it - the spoils of battle.
         (he chuckles dryly)   Now where's that drink?

TED: It's coming, Alf.   The spoils of battle you say.   Yes,
         you could call it that - the spoils of battle.

         (He examines the scarred malalignment of
         his knuckles)

         That really is something now, isn't it - the spoils of
         battle.

ALF: That's what I said - the spoils of battle.

TED: Well, we've all killed and suffered in our time.
         Dempsey too, Alf.   Billy Miske died.

ALF: Did he now?

TED: Ay, though each man kills differently.   Each man....

HONEY: To his own particular weapon.

TED: (surprised)   Oh - and what was yours may I ask?

ALF: Who cares, damn it, who cares!   Isn't it enough to
         know that every man-jack alive has done his fair bit
         of dirty work without wanting to know what he did it
         with?

TED: I merely asked, Alf, because some day a man might
         have to account for it - I mean in front of the Lord.

ALF: (snorts)   Now you look here.   If the Lord's all that
         he's cracked up to be then he's going to understand
         our predicament.

TED: That's hardly the point.   It can rust on your conscience.

ALF: Then unrust it with a bit of honest lubrication - that's
            what I say.   After all said and done, we've all done
            our duty and as far as I'm concerned I'd do it again!

                    (He bangs on the armrests)

TED: Then may the Lord have mercy on us.

                    (Pause as ALF tugs at the sleeve of HONEY'S
                    jacket - points at TED)

ALF: Now there stands a man who once shot a man!

TED: Alf, I must be getting up.

ALF: No, you stay and keep us company for awhile.

TED: (to HONEY)   It really weren't no fault of mine, you
            know.   I was deputy sheriff then in a one-horse Texan
            cattletown where the Mexes used to get loco on hemp
            and tequila - razing and thieving and lifting the skirts
            of women.   Naturally I had a job to do.

                    (He frowns, staring hard at his knuckles as
                    DOT enters with port and glass)

ALF: And what have you been doing - making it?

                    (DOT doesn't reply but begins to pour)

            Fill them all up while you're at it and get one for
            Hinds' pal.

DOT: But Alf.....

ALF: Please do as I say.   It's time we done a bit of
            celebrating in this house.

DOT: Yes, but the doctor said .....

ALF: Damn the doctor.   This is an occasion, I tell you.
            It's not every day of the week that we're blest with
            a new share who pays on the dot.

                    (Resigned, DOT goes to the sideboard for
                    glasses)

TED: And you have one too, Dottie.

DOT: Well, perhaps just a sip.

            (She begins to fill glasses)

ALF: Blasted doctors have been bothering this leg o' mine
            for thirty odd years and now they want to start in on
            my liver - well I won't have it, I tell you.

DOT: You've got nothing to complain about Alf - you've had
            the best treatment in the country.

ALF: They had me down at the Royal Free, Ted, where
            some old shyster stuck a needle in my side, but I got
            my own back all right.   I had a rattling good cough at
            the time and do you know what I did? Well, when it
            was all over I leaned forward in a most confidential
            way and coughed right in her face.

TED: (raising his glass)   To the ladies - God bless them.

            (They all murmur 'To the ladies' and drink)

ALF: (squinting at his held, half empty glass)   Ah, bit of
            body in that, Ted, bit of body.

TED: Ay.

ALF: Colour though reminds me a bit of them blood trans-
            fusion bottles they use in hospitals.

            (Silence)

            Lined up they were in rows - just bags of the stuff.
            Yet blokes still bled to death - thousands of them.

            (Pause)

            Just mashed into the mud and all them useless bottles
            left looking pretty on a shelf.

            (he gulps his drink)

            Now I wonder what those doctors would have to say
            about that, eh?

TED: Alf, did I ever tell you about the terrible end of
            Griffo - one time the best little fighter in the game?

ALF: (raising himself)   You'll have to save it, Ted, I'm
            afraid.   (he points to the door)   I've got to go out
            there, mind you, and all on account of that rotten

tea. If I had my way I'd burn down those damned
plantations. Ted, you'll have to give me a hand.

(TED takes his arm and they move across
the room)

It's the curse of the nation and it goes through you,
you know, worse than bitter.

(At the door he faces DOT)

Why in blazes can't we drink coffee in this house?

(They exit)

DOT: (to HONEY) I hope you don't mind their talk?

(HONEY shakes his head)

At least it doesn't get worse. By the way, I ought to
mention the fact that Hinds is a bit deaf - I hope you
won't mind?

(HONEY shakes his head)

That's good because Mr. Lister, for instance, doesn't
like people unless as he says they're all of a piece. I
suppose that bad leg of his makes him feel that way
together with what he had to put up with in the war. He
never did get over that - among other things. Still,
Hinds is all right.

(HONEY closes his eyes)

Tell me, are you very tired?

HONEY: No no - it's all right.

DOT: And please don't mind Mr. Lister. He tells the same
old stories over and over again of how men died like
flies and things like that. Personally I don't understand it. I mean .... why do people have to pick on
the rotten things to remember as if nothing else ever
happened to them?

HONEY: I suppose it's because some people have no luck.

DOT: Hinds too. He goes on about Korea as if he'd never
been anywhere else and Ted's always talking about the
shocking things that happened in America. Really, I
don't follow it. Women of course can be bad enough

what with their ailments and all, but men... well
men are just like kids. You know... sort of out to
prove... to pretend ... (she falters)

HONEY: How invulnerable they are to defeat and death?

DOT: How do you mean - I don't get it.

HONEY: It's not worth getting. In the end one dies - that's all,
           but people won't face up to it.

DOT: Then why all this talk about how men died instead of
           how they lived... like ... like... just how they lived
           would do even if most of them had to live like limpets
           on a rock. I mean, it's being alive that counts, isn't
           it - not how people died and why?

HONEY: It would depend I think of your point of view.

DOT: Yes, but why should they, that's what I want to know.
           I mean ... surely there are other things worth
           thinking about?

HONEY: That would still depend on your point of view.

DOT: That's all very well but point of view or no point of
           view it doesn't make sense. It's sickening.

HONEY: I expect it would be if you're an optimist.

DOT: But I'm not an optimist or anything else. I just believe
           in keeping afloat if you follow me; that's all.

                   (As they look at each other HONEY bends
                   forward as if to speak confidentially)

ALF: (off) Dot, get another bottle, will you?

                   (HONEY settles back as flustered, DOT bends
                   towards him)

DOT: What were you going to say?

                   (HONEY bends forward again)

ALF: Dot, where's that confounded drink?

                   (HONEY shakes his head as DOT sighs and
                   rummages in the sideboard. TED helps
                   ALF to his chair)

ALF: Don't go pushing me, Ted, as if I was a helpless
            pedestrian.

            (DOT puts a bottle of port on the table)

            Ah!

DOT: There - it's the last one.

ALF: My word, you had that pretty well hidden, didn't you.
            And it can't be the last one.

DOT: Well it is.

ALF: Then I'm being diddled.   Ted, you heard what she
            said - said it was the last one.

DOT: She's the cat's mother.

ALF: She has the hide, mind you, the bare-faced hide to tell
            me it's the last one when only last week I hobbled out
            on me own - practically out on the beg - to get half
            a dozen from O'Keefe. Well, it's not half good enough
            enough and I've the idea, mind you, that someone here
            has been drinking me out of house and home until I'm
            down, like now, to the last frigging dregs.

DOT: It was a fortnight Tuesday since you went down to
            O'Keefes.

ALF: Now don't you start telling me my business - it was
            last week.   Furthermore, if it wasn't for this unfort-
            unate predicament of mine ...

            (He slaps his leg)

DOT: Is it hurting you?

ALF: Of course it's hurting me.

DOT: Then it's because you drink too much.

ALF: It's the only blessed thing that gives me pleasure in
            this house and yet someone here is out to get at me.
            And we were going to celebrate.

TED: We will, Alfie boy.   I'm going right up this minute
            to bring down something to warm up the cockles of
            that leg.

ALF: Ah, you do that, Ted, you do that - it's got a thirst tonight let me tell you.

DOT: I wish you wouldn't, Ted. You know what the doctor said. He said if Alf overdid it he could have a stroke.

ALF: Ah, you'd like that now, wouldn't you?

DOT: God's will be done.

ALF: (mimicking her) God's will be done. Did you hear what she said, Ted?

TED: She's right, Alf.

ALF: And I'm wrong, am I?

TED: Why go begging the question - what good can it do?

ALF: It can clear the bloody deck - that's what it can do.

DOT: You can't be right all the time, you know.

ALF: And why not?

TED: Because it isn't human.

ALF: Bah! - you're against me.

TED: You know that's not true.

ALF: In my own home, in my own backyard of all places. Well that's not human either and if it weren't for this ... this... predicament of mine....

TED: Now you just sit tight, Alfie boy, and I'll be back with something for that predicament of yours.

ALF: Ah, Ted, I don't know what I'd do without you, really I don't.

> (He dryly chuckles and drops his head onto his chest - begins to doze. As TED goes out he reassures DOT with a squeeze on the arm. At that moment HONEY rises and walks towards his bag)

DOT: Won't you stop for a cup of coffee? After all, Hinds shouldn't be long now.

HONEY: Thank you, but in the circumstances.......

DOT: Please!

                 (Nervously she looks away as HONEY stares
                    at her)

        It'll please Alf, you see - make him feel that every-
        one's sort of with him if you know what I mean. He's
        like a kid really ... loves to show off a bit in front of
        strangers... I mean ... people.

                 (Shyly she faces him)

        Now please stay.

HONEY: (clenching and unclenching his hands)   I shouldn't.

DOT: But why not?   After all, we're all friends here.

HONEY: Of course... it's not that.

DOT: Then.... what?

HONEY: It's just that I should rest and relax a bit.

DOT: Well that's easily fixed. You go and sit down again
        and make yourself comfortable while I go and finish
        the washing up.

                 (HONEY nods and sits down again as DOT
                    bends over ALF)

        Alf, do you want your leg rubbed or something?

ALF: I'm all ri...

                 (DOT takes a handkerchief from her sleeve
                    and wipes his lips)

DOT: Don't go nodding off now - we're going to have some
        coffee soon.

                 (ALF grunts and DOT turns to HONEY)

        All that talk about the war has tired him out.

HONEY: Our father's war.   Doesn't he ever mention the
        other one?

DOT: Not if he can help it because he wasn't in it you see.
        He had to sit at home twiddling his thumbs which put
        his back up proper because apart from that bad leg

of his he's quite an able bodied man.   So if you don't mind, please don't mention that other war because he likes to think you see that it never really happened. It's one of the reasons why Hinds rubs him up the wrong way because Hinds got himself a perforated eardrum in Korea, and though he's never let on to me I think Mr. Lister's a bit envious of that because he always cuts Hinds short when ever he mentions it.

       (Pause)

I hope I'm not talking too much?

HONEY: No.... talk if you want to.

DOT: You only say that because you're.... a gentleman.

       (HONEY stands and glances longingly at his bag)

HONEY: I really think I ought to be going.

DOT: Have I said anything?

HONEY: Of course not.   It's just that.....

DOT: Look, I'll go up if you like and pull down the covers. It's a nice room.   Hinds likes it though he just hates being alone.

HONEY: Does he?

DOT: Don't you?

HONEY: No.... at least, I don't think so.

DOT: (folding her arms and rubbing her shoulders)   Then you're lucky.

      (She turns as TED enters carrying two bottles of liquor)

TED: Now here's the promised bounty.

      (He puts bottles on the table)

DOT: I wish you hadn't Ted.   You know what the doctor said about his liver: it won't stand abuse much longer.

TED: It's good red wine, Dottie, and won't hurt him a bit. In fact we can all do with a bit of cheering up.

DOT: Well he's dozed off again so you'd better not disturb
          him.

TED: Ay.

DOT: And please stay awhile, Mr. Honey.   The coffee won't
          be long.

          (HONEY nods as she turns and goes out to
            kitchen)

TED: Now there's a fine woman for you... a fine one. Old
          Alf here though has gone climbing up the rainbow.

HONEY: To the war.

TED: Ay, to the war. He's never forgotten it.

HONEY: Does he want to?

TED: Why should he?

HONEY: Because it belongs to a past that should be permitted
          to die.

TED: Weren't you ever in a war?

HONEY: Why do you ask?

TED: Because who's ever to really know what happened to
          Alf in that time?

HONEY: Who's ever to know what really happens to anyone?

TED: True - but the difference is I know this man and even
          if it's a fact that I can't really know what happened to
          him at least I can ride along with him. No harm in
          that the way I see it.

HONEY: By reliving the past? What do you hope to gain,
          Mr. Ward?

TED: Confidence and friendship for a start. The point is -
          I wasn't even at the war but Alf thinks I was and that's
          all that matters now because it makes him feel a part
          of things if you see what I mean. You see, when a
          man gets on..

          (HONEY smiles and glances at his bag)

          Oh, you can smile, son, but it'll happen to you too.

Hell man, you'll want to know what happened to the self who set out with two free mits and a heart full of hope with plans to knock the world into a cocked hat and didn't but got bushed and knocked about instead, yet all that's not going to stop you from wanting to know what happened to the lost pieces, but like the rest of us you'll find the return's a darned side tougher trek than you bargained for, so you'll want to stop off somewhere on the way. Alf, you see, stopped off at the war.

HONEY: But there are those of us who endeavour... not to stop off.

TED: Oh, you will sooner or later. That's one of the compensations for being so old that you can take time out to look behind.

HONEY: Wouldn't it be wiser to face... your death?

TED: Look, I'll skate along just as I am not caring a fig for my death. And if it should come today or tomorrow - O.K. - so let it come - I'm ready for it.

(Shaking his head TED begins to pace the room then spins around on HONEY who stands and glances at his bag)

But I'll tell you one thing, son - death has the face of a woman!

(As HONEY stares at him, TED hunches his shoulders and comes close to him)

Yes, you heard what I said - a face that once seen can never be forgotten: a face you never saw the likes of. A face I can't quite describe but a face, by God, that can never be forgotten. I was on a sick-bed at the time in Texas with a fever pouring out of me when I looked up and saw a figure by the bedrail smiling in a way you've never seen man smile. T'was then that I figured it weren't no man's face at all but the face of a mad and terrible and incredibly beautiful woman.

HONEY: Beautiful?

TED: Ay, she was beautiful all right.

HONEY: But mad?

TED: Mad in a way I never saw before. Yes, you could say she was mad.

HONEY: And you were afraid?

TED: At first I was but not later on when I knew I had the beating of her. Then she was really beautiful.

HONEY: But terrible?

TED: Terrible because she wanted to win. Old Dempsey was a bit like that. I can recall the terribleness of his face after Firpo put him on the deck - you never saw such a look in all your born days. So I recognised her look when it came.

HONEY: And she came only... the once?

TED: Frankly putting it I wouldn't call her 'she'. The figure was that of a lean and crafty welterweight: Benny Leonard you might say was built the same. But what I want to say is this - let's knock the top off one of these bottles here and drink to life.

(OFF - a slamming door)

Hullo, maybe that's your mate now.

HONEY: Who?

TED: Hinds.

(The hall door handle rattles and the next moment MOLL enters. She is a tall, thin, still fairly attractive woman of about forty. There is nothing slovenly about her at all. As she glances at the Company TED beams)

Why Moll, old girl.... how's the boy?

MOLL: He's asleep, thank God.

(She blinks at HONEY and automatically touches her hair)

TED: Moll, this is Mr. Honey - the new share with Hinds.

HONEY: How do you do?

MOLL: Fine, thank you.

(To TED)

Why didn't anyone tell me we were entertaining - I
would have put something decent on.

TED: You look just fine as you are, Moll dear. Now come
            on in and take it easy.

MOLL: (studying HONEY) You know, if you don't mind me
            saying so you remind me of someone I've seen in the
            pictures.

TED: Ah, Moll, it's sure nice. . . .

MOLL: Shush - please Ted.   Now let me think.

                (She steps closer)

It was someone I saw in one of those old re-runs - at
the Rialto it was... now let me think... I've almost
got it ... yes, of course... Pat O'Brien before he got
too bald - as he was for instance in ANGELS HAVE
DIRTY FACES.

TED: Angels, Moll?

MOLL: Of course. They were the dead-end kids and Cagney
            was Rocky remember. Bogart was the gangster and
            Pat O'Brien the priest.   Pat O'Brien had to plead
            with Rocky to squeal when in the chair.

TED: The hot seat.

                (MOLL closes her mouth with a snap.
                Discreetly TED begins to open the liquor)

MOLL: Pat O'Brien had to plead with Rocky to squeal when in
            the chair for the sake of the kids, see, so that they
            could know that he was yellow.   God, the suspense
            was awful. They showed him in close-ups strapped
            to the chair.   Then he squealed. He yelled. God,
            he was worse than Susan Hayward.

TED: I once saw a man get the gas treatment.

MOLL: You would!

TED: And believe me, I'd rather be scorched any day.

MOLL: You'd squeal - just like Rocky did.

TED: Then they'll have to hang me, I'm afraid.

MOLL: You're too old even for that.

(TED grunts and raises a glass of wine to ALF)

TED: Well, here's to you, old soldier.

MOLL: Old soldier nothing. Why don't you try and make him
          forget the war instead of encouraging him by calling
          him .... old soldier?

TED: It's a term of affection, Moll, that's all.

MOLL: A term of affection! Why, look at him!

TED: So what.... he looks all right to me.

MOLL: Of course he would because you're two peas out of the
          same pod - an old soldier and an old pug who do
          nothing all night but kill some poor wretch over and
          over again. Have you heard them, Mr. Honey?

(HONEY smiles)

          Why, Ted's more crazy about a left hook than some
          people are about vegetable marrows.

(She giggles)

TED: Now come off it, Moll. Alf's been a good friend to
          me as you know.

MOLL: Oh you both make me sick. They'd go on hanging
          together like rotten fruit, Mr. Honey, if someone
          didn't come along sometimes and shake them down.

TED: Now look Moll - if it's Jim you're worried about I'll
          go right up this minute and sit with him.

MOLL: You'll do nothing of the kind, thank you - he's asleep.

(She grimaces as she looks at ALF)

          For God's sake will you look at him! Now tell me,
          what does he remind you of, Mr. Honey?

HONEY: No one. I mean ... he's just asleep, isn't he?

MOLL: Is he? Well I'll tell you what he reminds me of -
a bald, horrid little Peter Lorre in THE BEAST WITH
FIVE FINGERS - a nasty, fat, little piano player!

   (Throwing back her head she breaks into
   laughter: HONEY, as though to shield
   himself, puts up his hands to his face and
   sways. TED steadies him)

TED: Moll, stop it, stop it, will you!

   (He helps HONEY to sit)

Listen, man, are you all right?

   (HONEY nods)

Why, you nearly fainted. Moll, what in blazes got
into you?

MOLL: What do you mean - what got into me? All I did was
laugh.

TED: Laugh? It was like cutting the air with a knife.

MOLL: Well he scared me.

TED: How could he scare you when he's dead to the world.

MOLL: I don't mean him - I mean Mr. Honey. He went all
white as if he was going to faint.

TED: Now then Moll.

   (He takes her hands)

You're nervous, that's all.

   (MOLL rips her hands away)

MOLL: Don't treat me like a child!

TED: God forbid.

   (He turns to HONEY and slowly shakes his
   head as DOT appears in the kitchen entrance)

DOT: Now what's going on in here?

TED: Nothing, Dottie. We were just laughing at one of
Moll's jokes.

MOLL: Joke nothing.

          (She points at HONEY)

          It was him almost fainting.

DOT: Oh.

TED: It was nothing, Dottie.

MOLL: Now you listen to me, Ted Ward. . . . .

DOT: Moll dear, I want you to help me in the kitchen.

MOLL: What, right away?

DOT: Please Moll.

MOLL: (begins to walk towards DOT)   All right then but let
me tell you that all I did was laugh when Mr.
Whatsisname in there went as white as a sheet and
nearly fainted.

DOT: (to the men) The coffee won't be long now.

          (She and MOLL enter kitchen. Their voices
          are heard for a few seconds and then fade)

TED: (drinking) You've got to pardon Moll, Mr. Honey.
She's highly-strung at times but that's all on account
of the boy. Sick, you know, and fatherless. Moll's
had the whole load of bringing him up on her own and
that makes for a pretty bundle of nerves. Drink?

          (HONEY shakes his head)

          Well you ought to have one and help clear the air a
bit.

          (He begins to pour HONEY a drink as LIGHTS
          DOWN ON STAGE - UP IN KITCHEN. DOT
          is standing watching the coffee percolate:
          MOLL is right behind her)

MOLL: Well I don't like the looks of him at all and I can't
understand you taking in anyone off the street like
that then inviting him to sit around like the star
boarder. You don't know, you know, he could be
anyone. Pulling that faint like he did.

DOT: All I know is that he's the new share with Hinds and that we can do with the extra.   Besides, he's a gentleman.

MOLL: And they're generally the worst because you don't know where you stand with them.   Remember how that Uncle Harry kidded everybody he was such a nice chap in SHADOW OF A DOUBT - that Joseph Cotton? Well, you know how he turned out what with sawing off the back step for Teressa Wright and all.   So you can't be too careful, you just can't.

DOT: But Moll, surely you've noticed....

MOLL: What?

DOT: It's hard to explain but there's something sweet and gentle about him which makes him seem different if you know what I mean.

MOLL: No I don't.   I tell you, Dot, you've got to take precautions.   After all, there's young Jim, you know.

DOT: Apart from that jaundice of his Jim's as safe as a nail in a board.

MOLL: Well, he'd better be.   I tell you, I don't like the look of him what with him nearly pulling that faint probably just to get our sympathy.   Anyway, where does he come from?

(DOT shrugs)

Don't shrug like that, I want to know.

DOT: Out there somewhere... I suppose.

MOLL: That's you all over saying 'out there' as if 'out there' was just around the corner.   Where is 'out there' - that's what I want to know.   'Out there' could be any- where: the lunatic asylum or jail or a deserted room full of squawking kids.

DOT: Now then Moll, there's no need to be suspicious.

MOLL: Oh Moll Moll Moll.   Moll's always the simple simon, isn't she?

DOT: You're nevous, that's all.

MOLL: I've a right to be.   How do you know that chap out

there's not nuts or a queer or something?

DOT: Queer in what way?

MOLL: For Pete's sake, Dot, don't be such an ignorant fool.
Now what are you smiling at?

DOT: Oh, I was just thinking.

MOLL: About him I hope.

DOT: Yes Moll, I was.

MOLL: What about?

DOT: O nothing much except how quiet and refined he is and
how he's the new share with Hinds.

                (MOLL sniffles and turns away)

MOLL: That's you all over having a go at me when all I was
trying to do was to put some sense into your head.
Frankly, I wouldn't trust him an inch.

DOT: I don't care Moll. He's the new share with Hinds and
that's that.

MOLL: By God, that's funny - Deafy and the Fairy - what an
intimate little twosome.   But I'll tell you one thing:
if he puts a hand on Hinds, Hinds'll kill him.

DOT: Now don't talk like that.

MOLL: It's true, and Ted will too - the bastard.

DOT: Moll!

MOLL: Are you afraid he'll hear?

DOT: No, for there's language enough in this house what
with Alf and Jim.

MOLL: You leave that sick boy upstairs out of it.

DOT: Then use some common decency towards that poor
man in there.

MOLL: Common decency - that's a good one - just what I
expected.

                (She quivers and bites her lip)

Well, if anything goes wrong in this house it's your responsibility. I don't want anything to do with it.

DOT: Moll dear, don't go on like that. Just before you came down we were going to have a little celebration.

MOLL: Celebration? Who died?

DOT: All right - so we weren't.

MOLL: There's old Alf asleep and Ted - what would he celebrate - his coming of age?

DOT: Please, Moll.

MOLL: Don't Moll me again, Dot. I'm tired.

DOT: I know that, dear.

MOLL: Then... then... don't.

(DOT murmurs and puts her arms about MOLL as LIGHTS DOWN - UP IN LIVING ROOM. TED is drinking and watching ALF doze as HONEY rises and goes to his bag, picks it up, tests the weight of it, and moves to the door. As he touches the handle TED swings around on him)

TED: Now wait a moment, where are you off to?

(Silence. HONEY turns the handle)

You can't run off now, son. The ladies are bringing some coffee in a moment.

(As HONEY opens the door TED goes and rests a hand on his arm)

Now come and sit down why don't you and take it easy. Damn it, man, awhile ago you nearly fainted.

HONEY: A temporary indiscretion.

TED: So you say but you listen to me.

HONEY: No, not to another word.

TED: I said - listen to me!

HONEY: I'm going.

TED: Hold it!

    (TED grabs HONEY'S hand which is holding
    the bag. HONEY tries to release himself
    but TED'S hold is too powerful. As the bag
    is finally wrestled from his grasp he pauses
    to stare at the old man)

HONEY: You had no right to do that.

TED: (shutting the door) No? Then if I hadn't, who had?

HONEY: Nobody.

TED: Nobody's a bum - a weeping, good-for-nothing bum
    and in my time I've met 'em all - every colour and
    breed under the sun, so forget about it.

    (He puts the bag down by the table and begins
    to pour drinks)

    All you need, son, is a drink and then you'll feel
    better. Here.

    (He hands HONEY a glass who accepts it
    mechanically and sips)

    Feel better?

HONEY: No.

TED: In that case you'd better sit quiet and wait till the
    ladies come.

HONEY: I should like to remind you that common to all paranoia
    is the lack of participant compassion.

    (TED grins widely and raises his glass to ALF)

TED: Then here's to you, old soldier.

    (LIGHTS DOWN - UP IN KITCHEN. DOT
    is seen with her arms about MOLL)

MOLL: Don't, you're hurting me.

    (DOT releases MOLL and returns to the stove)

DOT: You're nervous, dear, just nervous.

MOLL: I can't help it.

DOT: If it's Jim you're worried about you can forget it. The doctor said he'd be quite all right if he stayed in bed.

MOLL: Oh, it's not Jim I'm worried about so much - it's just that chap in there acting like he did. All I did was laugh and he nearly passed out.

DOT: Just forget about him Moll. I've noticed lately that you haven't been looking yourself. Is that Hitchens fellow bothering you again?

MOLL: Well what if he has?

DOT: Next time we'll call the police, that's what.

MOLL: For Pete's sake, Dot, I'm old enough.

DOT: Look what he did to the Nixon girl.

MOLL: They couldn't prove a thing.

DOT: Used an instrument, didn't he?

MOLL: For crying out loud, how do I know?

DOT: Well he did - her mother told me.

MOLL: That old bag of jealous wind. Anyway, he won't touch me that way.

DOT: I should hope not - Alf would have a fit.

MOLL: (laughing) By Jesus, so would I!

DOT: Anyway, you be careful, Moll.

MOLL: Course I will. Anyway, he's not so bad.

DOT: How do you mean .... he's not so bad?

MOLL: Dunno exactly but I sort of have the idea. You know, when you come to think of it he isn't half so bad really. Actually I ran into him when I went to the butchers and he asked me to meet him later on tonight for a drink. I said I might - you know, you have to do that, and he looked, you know, when he spoke - just a bit like William Holden in PICNIC - sort of... sexy-interesting but not in a mean way.

DOT: Oh, Moll.

MOLL: But he did and all the time I though he was more the
         Rod Steiger type.

DOT: I've told you before and I'll tell you again. You ought
         to get hold of Ted now while he's still hale and hearty.
         He'd be a good provider and kind to you and he loves
         young Jim.

MOLL: But I couldn't bear the thought of him.... touching
         me .... Dot.

DOT: For fifteen solid pounds a week any middle-aged
         woman with a fatherless son could bear it.

MOLL: There you go again - making out I'm through.

DOT: Well be nice to him, Moll - he's as keen as mustard.

MOLL: (sniffling)   That's what I'm afraid of.

                  (LIGHTS DOWN - UP IN LIVING ROOM.
                  ALF dozes: HONEY rests in his chair and
                  appears also to sleep. TED drains the last
                  of a bottle of wine and begins to pace the
                  room. Suddenly he stops in front of HONEY:
                  studies him intently)

TED: Tell me, now how is it, how is it that you - an utter
         stranger, can waltz into a place and take up a privil-
         eged position without declaring yourself one iota when
         all the time you could be ... our enemy, yes, our
         enemy. Let me tell you, son, that in the old days a
         man couldn't do that - he had to give an account of
         himself: just that - name, last address, occupation,
         history of antecedents, service record, marital
         status, health and civil history - stuff like that.
         After all now, after all, Moll had a bit of a turn over
         you and all because she might have seen - as women
         have the knack to do sometimes - had seen something
         pretty wrong beneath your skin.

                  (He shakes his head)

         After all, who knows here who you are and where you
         came from and what's your business and where you're
         going? Maybe you'll even tell me, senator, that it's
         none of my business and I'll buy it because you're
         right but all the same there's women in this house and
         a cripple and a sick boy and a share you've never seen
         before. For the sake of the record, senator, I think
         you ought to split a bit and talk to me.

(Impulsively he taps HONEY on the knee)

Now look here, senator, wake up ... you hear me...
wake up!

      (As HONEY doesn't move, TED frowns
      and scratches his head... mumbles)

Man must be as cold as a cod.

      (Suddenly taking HONEY'S nose between
      his fingers he squeezes it)

Now, wake up, damn it, or I'll cut off your air!

      (He stares incredulously at the seated figure)

Now you must have felt that, senator, you must have.

      (He shakes him)

Now come on, son, tell me, tell me that you felt it.

      (Silence)

All right, so go on playing the fox - I'll find a way,
you see if I don't.

      (He forges a cup with his hands and squeezes
      them together)

Now speak up or I'll take your manhood between my
hands and ruin yer!

      (Suddenly ashamed he drops his hands and
      shakes his head)

All you've got to do, son, is to tell me who you are
and where you came from and then you can go on
riding out of town - no harm in that, is there? Then
later on, well I'll tell you what we'll do - we'll
celebrate.

      (As HONEY remains silent TED suddenly
      leans forward and takes him by the lapels)

Now you listen to me, you squib, do you hear. Who
the hell do you think you are coming in here and
accepting our goddamned hospitality when all the time
you could be ...

                    (LIGHTS UP IN KITCHEN.   MOLL is
                    seen in the entrance holding the coffee pot)

MOLL: Ted!

                    (Guiltily TED releases HONEY and turns
                    sheepishly)

TED: I was.... just trying to wake him.   It seems he's
            fainted.

MOLL: What... again?

                    (She puts the pot on the table and comes
                    forward)

TED: Must have.

MOLL: Lord, he does look pasty.   Have you tried slapping his
            face?

TED: I ... no.   I was just shaking him.

MOLL: Then for goodness sake slap his face.

TED: (staring at his hands)   I.... can't.

MOLL: What do you mean you can't?

TED: Because ... it's a woman's job.

MOLL: Then hit him why don't you!

TED: Moll, there's no need to get upset.   Believe me, I'll...

MOLL: Oh stop gabbing and do something.

                    (With fumbling fingers TED loosens HONEY'S
                    necktie then begins to rub his wrists)

TED: He's ... out like a light.

MOLL: (sniffing)   Drunk you mean - the pair of you.

TED: All I did was shake him.

MOLL: You bloody men are all alike.   I'm going for Dot.

TED: Now hold it, Moll.

MOLL: You hold it!

(She goes to kitchen entrance)

DOT!

DOT: (off)   What is it?

MOLL: Just come in here a moment, will you.

DOT: (off)   You know I'm busy, Moll, what is it?

(She comes to kitchen entrance and sees HONEY)

Oh dear.

(She goes forward)

What... what's happened?

TED: Dunno, Dottie, but I think he's fainted and I was...

MOLL: You were shaking him.

TED: Of course I was shaking him, I told you that.

MOLL: If you had shaken him any harder his teeth would have fallen out.

TED: I know I'm strong for my age but then......

MOLL: Yeah, just like Lon Chaney Junior in MICE AND MEN.

DOT: Oh shut up the both of you.

(She leans over HONEY)

MOLL: Well, if I'm going to be insulted...

(TED shakes his head at her and puts a hand on her arm.   Restrained, MOLL nibbles her lips as she watches DOT rub HONEY'S hands)

DOT: It's all right, Mr. Honey, it's all right.... you're quite safe here, you're quite safe.   Now come on, it's all right now, it's all right.....

MOLL: For God's sake, Dot, do something!

DOT: I'm ... trying to.

TED: Hadn't we better send for a doctor?

DOT: No!

> (Pause as they watch her stroke HONEY'S
> forehead)

He must have had a bit of a shock or something. He's
quite cold.... almost.

TED: It could be hunger, Dot.

DOT: No, I don't think so.

> (Pause as she soothes his forehead)

I can't help thinking that he reminds me of.....
someone.

MOLL: Who?

DOT: Saint John if you want to know - there's a picture of
him in that stained-glass window at All Saints.

MOLL: Dot, don't be such a romantic fool. Just slap his face
and be done with it.

DOT: He's... all right now.

> (HONEY stirs and as he tries to rise DOT
> gently pushes him back)

No, you rest a tick.

> (HONEY sighs and slumps back)

MOLL: I tell you, if he's off again I'll scream.

TED: (catching MOLL's arm) Now keep to him, Dottie.

> (HONEY stirs again and stares about him)

DOT: There now... feeling all right?

MOLL: The best thing you can do is to get up and walk about.
Go on, get up and do something, don't just sit there.

DOT: Moll, let him be.

HONEY: Perhaps you are right.

MOLL: Of course I am - now go on - get up and walk.

HONEY: (not moving) Yes.

TED: (chuckling) I guess you were tanked, son - on one lousy glass.

MOLL: Drunk - the pair of you.

HONEY: So that was it.

MOLL: So that was what?

HONEY: Nothing.

DOT: Tell us, Mr. Honey.

HONEY: (looking into DOT'S face) That I was resting....
floating... had arrested anguish.

TED: That was good booze, son.

MOLL: (shaking off TED'S arm. Don't forget how you were,
Ted Ward.

(TED grins sheepishly and tries to take her
hand. She slaps his fingers)

DOT: You sit still, Mr. Honey, and I'll get you something to
eat and drink.

HONEY: Please don't bother.

DOT: But it's no bother. You've been asleep.

HONEY: Yes, I suppose so.

MOLL: What do you mean ; you suppose so? You either were
or you weren't.

HONEY: It was as though I was under ice - frozen.

DOT: That was only a bad dream. We all have them.

MOLL: You're not kidding. I once dreamt that Alf there had
two heads which he kept going all the time about that
leg of his and the war.

DOT: Well anyway it's time I woke him. But you sit quiet
for a moment, Mr. Honey, and then we'll have our
coffee.

> (As she goes and shakes ALF by the shoulder
> he awakes with a start)

ALF: Now what the... what the... blazes (he groans)

TED: Alf, old son, is it the leg again?

ALF: Leg be damned. It's.... it's... this confounded head
         of mine, that's what.

DOT: (pouring coffee) Oh dear, it would have to be.

ALF: Now that's enough out of you.

DOT: Do you want an aspirin?

ALF: Na-ow, what for, what for?

DOT: For your head.

MOLL: Which one?

ALF: What the hell do you mean by that remark?

DOT: Stop it both of you and let's drink our coffee.

ALF: Then tell her to keep her remarks to herself.

> (MOLL pulls a wry face as ALF moans and
> holds his head)

DOT: For heaven's sake what's wrong with you?

> (ALF shakes his head)

MOLL: The cat's taken his tongue - for once.

TED: It's his poor old head.

MOLL: So he says though you can be sure that if it wasn't that
         end it would be the other.   Dot, go and get him an
         aspirin so we can be left in peace.

> (DOT goes to drawer in sideboard)

Head indeed. He ought to have my head to know what
aches and pains are with all I've got to put up with
what with that sick boy up there and the mess he makes
and then having to cope with this.

> (She grimaces as DOT offers ALF an
> aspirin.   He shakes his head)

DOT: Now why not?

> (As ALF doesn't answer she puts the tablet
> into her own mouth)

MOLL: Good for you, Dottie - at least you need it.

TED: Ah, poor old Alf.

MOLL: Poor old Alf nothing.   It's Dot you ought to feel sorry
             for slaving away like she does while old soldier sits
             there like the Queen and barks his orders.

TED: Now come off it, Moll.

MOLL: Don't you start Molling me in that tone of voice, please.

DOT: Now stop it both of you.

ALF: (Thumping the armrests)   Then leave me alone!

> (Pause as all stare at him but HONEY who
> gazes longingly at his bag)

TED: Now that I would say is a mouthful.

> (He nods at the women and begins to drink
> his coffee)

MOLL: Well!

DOT: Alf, please try and pull yourself together.   There's
             Mr. Honey over there.....

ALF: Then get off my back.   Why, what with this confounded
             leg o' mine....

DOT: I though you said it was your head?

> (MOLL snorts)

ALF: So it was at first but when you all started in on me
             this... this... poor old leg o' mine started to throb
             like a toothache, damnit, and... and... you know
             what it does... does to me... grips me like a shark..
             all bite,.... and, and, I'll tell you what... it could do
             now with a bit of a rub seeing that you're all finished
             having a go at me.

DOT: Alf, why didn't you say so?

ALF: Because... I didn't want to bother you.

      (DOT rests a hand on his shoulder. MOLL,
      watching ALF petulantly shake it off, snorts
      with disgust and hurriedly goes out by the
      hall door. Slams it. Worriedly DOT faces
      TED)

DOT: Ted, see that she's all right, will you. She's over-
      wrought.

TED: I will, Dottie, I will.

      (He goes out after MOLL)

ALF: (relaxing) If you ask me that Moll's got an itch in
      her drawers.

DOT: (contemplating the pot and cups) She's tired - that's
      all. She's been up with Jim for hours.

      (She sighs and collects the cups)

      I'll be back soon, Mr. Honey. You just keep Mr.
      Lister company for a minute.

      (She goes out as ALF studies HONEY who is
      staring at his bag)

ALF: I say.

      (Silence. ALF coughs. Silence)

      I say there... anyone at home?

      (He chuckles)

      Now look here, I said... is there anyone at home?

HONEY: (facing him) It's time I was going.

ALF: Oh..... where?

HONEY: Upstairs.

ALF: Oh, you do, do you? Why?

HONEY: Because I'm the new share.

ALF: So you say.   Now who are you?

HONEY: The new share.

ALF: I know all about that, I mean your name.

HONEY: I've told you.

ALF: Friend of Hinds?

HONEY: No.

ALF: Protestant?

                (HONEY doesn't answer)

                Who said you could share anyway?

HONEY: I've already paid you a week's rent for that privilege.

ALF: Never mind the details - I want to know all about you.

HONEY: Why?

ALF: Because I've the right to know just who it is who buys
            a bed in my house, that's why.

HONEY: (rising and moving towards his bag) I don't need your
            bed if it comes to that.

ALF: Now wait a tick - don't go sweating yourself.

HONEY: I've waited too long as it is.

ALF: It's that ruddy Hinds.   He's no consideration for any-
            one but his own miserable self.   I'm going to get rid
            of him.

HONEY: Thank you for your hospitality.

ALF: Now calm down and don't go upsetting yourself.   After
            all, you're not Irish, are you?

HONEY: (picking up his bag)   I'm going.

ALF: Put that blooming thing down - it makes me nervous.
            Now go on.

                (HONEY slowly puts the bag down)

                That's better.   Now sit down and tell me your troubles.

HONEY: Troubles?

ALF: What's worrying you.

HONEY: Nothing is worrying me.

ALF: Sit down for Pete's sake.   Now go on.

           (HONEY slowly sits opposite)

           So nothing is worrying you, eh?   Then you're a lucky
           man.

HONEY: It isn't always a question of luck but of insight.

ALF: Insight be damned - it's luck!   You're young, aren't
           you?   You've got your health and strength, haven't
           you?   And you've paid your way - why shouldn't you
           be lucky?

HONEY: As I said.   It's not always a question of luck but....

ALF: So you said, so you said, but then you're a weeper, a
           moaner, a bloody down-in-the-mouth. I know your
           type.   Get a few drinks inside of you and you're
           ready to cry on the world's shoulder. But then there's
           a reason for that.

HONEY: They say there's a reason for everything. I say they
           lie.

ALF: You're afraid, that's what you are - afraid.

HONEY: Afraid?

ALF: That's right - afraid.   (pause)   Like me.

HONEY: Like you?

ALF: Yes. Like me.

HONEY: But you bear your fear and by doing so you control it,
           so I don't see.......

ALF: But how could you see - you're not inside my head,
           are you? - you're not inside my skin? How the
           devil could you see, how could anyone see?   And
           how do you know I bear it, that it doesn't... this fear
           I've got... that's got me... tortures me to the point
           of... makes my life what it is ... a living hell!

                    (Gushing through his teeth he begins to nurse
                    his leg)

HONEY: I begin to understand.

ALF: You know, as soon as I saw you I said to myself, now
                there's someone I can talk to. Like when you said or
                hinted rather that my fear sprang from this old leg o'
                mine. Now that's what I call ... perspicacity.

                    (He chuckles at his preposterous use of that
                    word then bends forward confidentially)

                But that's not the half of it. Old Ted and the wife
                want me to have it off and do you want me to have
                to tell you why? Well I'll tell you - because they
                would see me helpless - that's why.

HONEY: But you have a very stubborn, a very remarkable leg.

ALF: So I've been told but then you listen to me. If it
                weren't for the fact that Hinds did a makeshift job on
                rubbing this old pin I would have had him out of here
                long ago. By the way, speaking of bad legs, what's
                your hands like.

HONEY: (rising and glancing at his hands) Weak.

ALF: That's all right but are they soft... soft?

HONEY: Yes.

ALF: In that case you had better give me a close look at
                them.

                    (He leans forward as HONEY inches back
                    gripping his thigh low down with one hand.
                    As the fingers twitch he suddenly cries out
                    and brushes it away with his other hand.
                    ALF gasps aloud and leans back in his chair)

                Gawd Almighty... what in blazes... do you think...
                you're... damn well doing?

HONEY: (bringing his hands together and locking them) Nothing.

ALF: Nothing! Jesus, man, you almost gave me the willies
                doing what you did. Why, talk about Hinds....

HONEY: I'm waiting for him.

(Unclasping his hands he holds them out in
front of him, trying to stay the trembling.
Fascinated, ALF watches)

ALF: Now look.... what... what the heck's going on?

HONEY: (slowly bringing his palms together) It's true you see
            - they are soft.

ALF: Well I've got to admit that I've never quite seen the
            likes of them but I suppose that's because you use
            lots of vaseline.   I keep telling Dot that - Mrs. Lister,
            you know, and Hinds whose hands are all red and
            crinkled with detergents - like a baby's bum.   Now
            hold 'em still, will you... that's right.   Ah!   You
            know, they might just do, you know, and if they do
            I'll use them all right, you see if I don't, and we'll
            have that Hinds set by the short hairs once and for all.
            Now look here, would you mind... giving... this old
            leg o' mine a rub: start around the calf and shin just
            to get the circulation going and then later on, now
            look, it might be more convenient if you squatted or
            knelt the same as Ted and Hinds.

            (HONEY slowly sinks to his knees as ALF
            rolls up his trouser leg)

            That's right... the carpet's soft... now use a gentle
            motion to begin with around the ankle now... now...
            wait a minute... what on earth... what the bloody
            heck... what the... what... what...

            (Alarmed, ALF watches HONEY'S hands
            begin to tremble as he tries desperately
            to control them.   As they are about to
            touch ALF'S flesh, he gives a moan and
            falls over on his side as ALF gasps and
            throws himself back in the chair)

            Dot!   Eh Dot!   Dot......!

                              CURTAIN

ACT TWO

> SCENE: The living room.

> TIME: Some minutes later.

> (HONEY is slumped in one of the chairs - the others grouped around him. TED loosens his necktie. DOT places a wet cloth on his fore-head. HONEY stirs....)

TED: There... I guess he's coming round.

ALF: And so he should. What the devil does he mean by fainting away in my house like a ... like a ... fainting saint?

TED: Ay, but he could be a diabetic.

MOLL: Why, do they faint at the drop of a hat?

TED: They will if their sugar's down.

MOLL: Tch-tch. Poor creature.

ALF: Sweetpretty creature - sweetpretty creature.

MOLL: Oh, drop dead, you.

ALF: You'd like that now, wouldn't you?

DOT: Please, don't go on arguing. Have some consideration for poor Mr. Honey.

ALF: You mean... Saint Honey - God's gutless wonder?

DOT: Never you mind who I mean. You know nothing... nothing. All you know is that he came here looking for a room like anyone else. For all you know he could be a ... saint... and yet you wouldn't know the difference between that and a truck driver.

ALF: Now you pipe down and listen to me. Saints - even if there were any - which there ain't, don't go fainting at the roll of a trouser cuff. All I did was to ask him to rub this old leg o' mine when he squawked and keeled over on the carpet as if he was hit. In my opinion he's nothing but....

DOT: I won't listen.

ALF: Oh yes you will. He's sick - that's what he is.
            Anyone who can't stand the sight of a bit of helpless
            flesh is sick or up to no damned good.

MOLL: So you had him down on the carpet in front of you, did
            you, just like Hinds and Ted and anyone else who'll do
            your dirty work?

ALF: (shocked) What on earth.... what in blazes... what
            ... are you suggesting?

MOLL: I'm suggesting that you ought to be ashamed of your-
            self. I'm also suggesting that it's disgusting.

ALF: Of all the damned infernal cheek! Is this my house
            or isn't it? What do you mean by butting your head
            into my personal affairs?

MOLL: I'll have you know I pay my way.

DOT: Shush... both of you. He's wakening, I think.

TED: Ay.

ALF: Sooner the better then so that he can vacate this
            blooming tomb. Why, talk about celebrating, Ted -
            it's more like a flaming wake!

TED: Ay.

DOT: Now just you keep quiet and leave him alone.

ALF: Leave him alone!

                    (He points dramatically at HONEY)

            You just tell him to leave me alone - to leave us all
            alone.

DOT: I'm not going to listen to you.

TED: Alf, all he's doing is waiting for Hinds.

ALF: What's Hinds got to do with him leaving us in peace?

DOT: Because he's the new share and has paid his way.

ALF: Then I'll give it back to him.

DOT: You can't.

ALF: What do you mean - I can't?   I'll have you know that
            I can and will.   There!

                        (Taking out his handkerchief he throws it at
                            her feet)

            That's what I think of you and him.

                        (DOT retrieves it and puts it on his lap)

DOT: You'll be needing this later on.

ALF: Blast yer!

                        (He throws the handkerchief behind his chair)

            Who do you think is the master of this house?

DOT: (retrieving the handkerchief)   You... of course.

                        (She returns the handkerchief to ALF's lap)

ALF: Then damn well remember it.

                        (Settling back in his chair he glowers about
                            him. Frowning, TED begins to pace the
                            room while MOLL glares at ALF with
                            disdain)

            Just you damn well remember it.

MOLL: You and that mouth of yours.   I don't understand why
            Dot keeps taking it from you.   I wouldn't.   It's no
            wonder Jim....

ALF: That boy of yours is no damned angel.

MOLL: Nor do I want him one.   All I want of him is to grow
            up clean.

ALF: (scoffing)   That's a good one.   Why, he's about as
            clean...

MOLL: As any kid if you'd only leave him alone.

ALF: (shocked)   Leave... him... alone!   What do you
            mean by .... leave him alone?

MOLL: You know very well what I mean.

ALF: Dottie, what does she mean by... leave him alone?

Does she mean.....

DOT: She means for you to keep a civil tongue in your head, that's all.

ALF: Then why can't she say what she means instead of casting aspersions on my character by telling me to leave him alone. If it was anyone else telling me to leave-him-alone in that tone of voice I'd serve him with a writ, by God I would. And I'd claim damages - substantial damages. I'd have a writ out all right - a bit fat writ. Sister-in-law or no sister-in-law I'd have her up in the dock!

DOT: As usual, Alf, you're making a mountain out of a molehill.

ALF: But you know how it is, how this poor old leg o' mine works me up. If only someone would give it a bit of a rub now and again it would be all right but then what does he do? I no sooner roll up my trousers than he squawks as if he was hit and keels over on the carpet.

MOLL: That leg of yours would be better off.

ALF: Of course, you'd like that now, wouldn't you - seeing me on my back helpless as a baby. Oh yes, I know you - I know the lot of you.

MOLL: Rubbish!

ALF: Yes, the lot of you.

TED: (downstage) Silence!

(All stare at him)

Yes, I mean it.

(Pause as he glares threateningly)

I've heard nothing in this house tonight but gabble: inconsequential, no-good, poisonous gabble. If you could only hear yourselves you'd be so ashamed as to want to bury your tongues.

MOLL: Of all the .... now you listen to me, Ted Ward.

TED: Later, Molly. Now it's my turn.

(MOLL takes a step forward but is restrained

by DOT)

Tonight we set out in all good faith to celebrate an occasion - for all we know the last celebration any of us will ever have. Yet what do we do? No, don't interrupt me, Moll.

(About to protest, MOLL closes her mouth with a snap)

Well, I'll tell you what we do. We sit and nag and scrap and try to blind each other with our own dirt for the sake of keeping some personal little world going around for if we didn't that little world would stop and fling us into such a vacumn there'd be no coming out of it. Or... we'd rot and die or even worse - we'd just terrify each other with our screaming silences. But don't get me wrong: I'm as bad as any of you. But in these last minutes I've been doing a bit of thinking. Awhile ago I reckoned that ... that man there

(He points to HONEY)

was somehow responsible for us all getting our tails up, me included.

ALF: Hear! Hear!

TED: But he wasn't!

(ALF subsides under the weight of TED'S glare)

Whatever that man is or isn't, he isn't responsible for our bitching at each other. Damn it, he's done nothing all evening but sit tight, faint, and wait for Hinds while we've gone out of our way to persecute him and each other.

DOT: Yes, it's true.

TED: You can drop that bleeding heart of yours, Dot - there's no saint here.

MOLL: Are you accusing me, Ted Ward, of persecuting that poor man?

TED: Not you alone, Moll. All of us.

MOLL: Then it's a lie - a rotten lie!

TED: (lifting his arms to her)   But Moll......

MOLL: Don't Moll me, you old fake - it was you who started
            it.   I saw how you were pulling him about when I
            brought in the coffee.   If I hadn't come in when I did
            there's no knowing what you would have done, and yet
            there you are coming the Holy Joe so as to square
            your conscience at our expense.

ALF: Hear!   Hear!

TED: All right then, all right. If it's as you say it is then
            may the Lord help us all.

                        (Pause as they feel embarrassed and collect
                         their thoughts.   DOT glances at the mantle-
                         piece clock)

DOT: Hinds is late.

MOLL: On purpose if you ask me.

ALF: Moll's right.   He's up to no darned good.

DOT: Don't start that now, Alf, you know nothing about it.

ALF: I know enough to know that the man is no darned good.
            Though I should say half a man what with that put-on
            deafness of his.

DOT: Just keep it to yourself - we don't want to hear.

ALF: Sneaking in and out of my house like a ferret.

DOT: That happens to be a matter of opinion.

ALF: Oh, well opinion has it that he sniffs around the skirts
            on every dirty corner.

DOT: He doesn't.   He goes to the Young Men's Welfare
            Association.

MOLL: Oh, that's a laugh - how to put a girl in the family
            way in three easy lessons.   He's what I would call
            .... cheap.

TED: (scowling)   For Chris' sake stop bitching and
            forget about Hinds.

(MOLL dabs at her nose and sniffles)

MOLL: What with all the bullies in this house it's a wonder
         that poor boy upstairs can sleep at all.   Not one of
         you think about him - not one of you.   He could be
         dead for all you cared.

(TED comes and pats her shoulder)

TED: Now now, Moll - that boy's got grit and guts.   He's
         a chip off you, old girl, a chip off you.

MOLL: Well I should hope so after what I've had to put up
         with.   He's just got to be like me.

TED: He will, Moll, he will - without the shadow of a
         doubt.

MOLL: I'm going to see that he gets every opportunity to
         better himself.

TED: He will, Moll, he will.

MOLL: And he's going to be educated at one of those good
         schools.

TED: Ay.

(He glares at ALF who snorts contemptuously)

MOLL: Poor little devil.   I've got to go to him.

(TED takes her arm)

TED: Now then, Molly, don't go upsetting yourself - the
         boy's asleep, isn't he?

DOT: Ted's right, dear.   Leave him alone now then later
         on take him up something nice to eat.   There's a
         cake out there.

TED: Ay, Dottie's right - let him be.

(MOLL sniffles and dabs at her nose)

ALF: For Gawd's sake.....

TED: Moll, don't love.

(MOLL sits and hides her face in her
handkerchief as TED surveys the group)

Now listen everybody - don't let's just sit here
crying down our noses as if we were at a wake -
life's too short for that.   And if we didn't have
the right reason to celebrate before we certainly
have one now.   Moll and I have decided to get
married just as soon as that boy up there is well.

> (DOT gives a cry of pleasure and embraces
> MOLL)

DOT: Oh Ted, that's the best news I've heard in ages. Moll
            dear, I'm so happy for you.

MOLL: (sniffling but trying to smile)   He went and asked me
            in the hall.

TED: Ay, and her answer was the sweetest sound I've ever
            heard.

MOLL: He took me by surprise.

TED: Tactics, old girl, tactics.

MOLL: Grabbing me like you did.

TED: With honourable intent, my dear.

MOLL: Well a man of your age ought to be more prudent.

> (They all laugh)

ALF: Dottie, girl, if you go out into the coal house and
            look under that pile of sacks in the corner you'll find
            a drop of the doings.   Go and get it and we'll wet
            the baby's head.

> (He chuckles as TED comes and pumps his
> hand.   Smiling, DOT goes out. Pause as
> the others take in HONEY slumped in his
> chair)

MOLL: If Mister Thingamejum has passed away I'll have a
            fit.

TED: He's resting that's all.

MOLL: Well it's unnerving.

ALF: You should have seen him squawk like a bird then
            keel over on the carpet just as soon as I showed him
            this old leg o' mine.

TED: Maybe he's thinking?

ALF: Now why would anyone want to waste his time with that kind of nonsense for? Where's it get them, that's what I want to know - where's it get them?

TED: Well, it got me Molly here.

                (He fondles MOLL'S shoulders. ALF
                grimaces and turns away)

MOLL: Don't you be too sure about that, Mister Everready. No woman's ever trapped unless she wants to be. In fact, I promised myself that as soon as Jim got off to a good scholl I'd go out and have some fun. In fact I know of a certain stock broker....

TED: Ugh-ugh, I know the type, Moll - big hairless boys smothered in eau-de-cologne who'll force-feed you at some hole-in-the-corner restaurant before conning you into some hole-in-the-corner-bedroom. If I was a woman I wouldn't call that fun: I'd call it the sweat shop.

MOLL: You sure you don't mean the sweet shop, dear?

TED: It would be beneath any decent woman's dignity even to think about it.

ALF: Take that elder Nixon girl for example. Fell for some great hulk on the Main Roads Board and ended up in a ditch.

MOLL: Serves her right. She didn't know when to come in out of the rain.

TED: Well, it's indecent, I tell you. Indecent.

MOLL: (laughing) What is - the Nixon girl ending up wet in a ditch or yours truly contemplating the sweets of the sweat shop?

TED: Now stop it, Moll, stop it.

MOLL: Oh dear, some day I'll tell you about that big white bull of a footballer on the Tenby Downs. (laughs)

ALF: Footballer, eh? Well let me tell you I had my fair bit of glory myself when that old club o' mine.....

MOLL: What club - Wormwood Scrubs? (she laughs)

ALF: You can laugh for all you damn well like but if it
          hadn't been for this leg o' mine I would have worn
          the white jersey.

MOLL: What a pity poor Saint Honey there can't join in the
          fun.

TED: As it is he's got more sense... down in some place
          where nothing can reach him.

MOLL: Well it bothers me I'll have you know because I don't
          believe he's all there if you know what I mean.
          There's something odd about him which I don't like
          at all. As I said to Dot earlier on, I don't think he's
          a real man at all.

DOT: (entering from kitchen with fresh glasses and a bottle)
          Now just forget about him. He's simply the new share
          with Hinds.

MOLL: That's all very well but have a look at him.

DOT: He's at peace with himself and that's something.

                    (She begins to pour)

MOLL: Well whether he is or whether he isn't is beside the
          point. I have my own life to live without the likes
          of him upsetting me.

DOT: If he did you can be sure he didn't mean to.

ALF: There she goes again - fussing over dirty washing.

MOLL: Dropping off like he does as if he owned the place.

DOT: Shush - he'll hear you.

MOLL: A good job then. I want him to hear me.

TED: Now then, Moll, ease up, old girl.

MOLL: Why do you have to be so two-faced for? One minute
          you're knocking him about and the next you're wanting
          to kiss his feet!

ALF: Talking about feet I'm going to get rid of that Hinds.
          Hullo, don't tell me the turtle's stirring?

DOT: Shush. Now please remember that this is a celebrat-
          ion.

(She begins to hand around the glasses)

Ted, this is yours.   Alf.   There Moll dear.

       (HONEY sits upright and slowly glances
       about him)

Now Mr. Honey... this is yours.

       (She offers him a glass)

HONEY: Thank you, but I shouldn't.

DOT: Of course you should. You see, Ted and Moll here
are going to get married and so we wouldn't dream
of celebrating without you now because, well, you
were here when it all happened as if luck or a blessing
had suddenly fallen on this house.

       (She faces the others)

Now isn't that so?

TED: Of course it is.   Now come on everybody - let's
toast the bride.

       (He holds his glass aloft)

MOLL: To be - I'll have you know.

ALF: (chuckling)   Once bitten, twice shy, eh Moll? But a
girl like you now....

MOLL: It's once bitten, twice bitten if you want to know.

TED: Now come on.... to the bride!

ALL: To the bride.

       (They drink)

ALF: (sings)
Oh happy days are here again
Happy days to cheer again
Happy.. happy days are here ag-ain. (chuckles)

DOT: (raising her glass to TED and MOLL)   To you Ted
and to you Moll.   May you both live happy ever after.

       (She is almost crying with happiness and
       touched, MOLL goes to her and puts an

                        arm about her)

TED: (slapping HONEY on the back)   Have I told you, son, that you and I are going to get as tight as boots tonight?

MOLL: Indeed you're not, mister irresponsibility. What about me?

TED: You Moll? Why, there's nothing you and I can't solve.

                        (He comes and throws his arms about her and she squeals - pushes him away. ALF drops his head on his chest and begins to doze: HONEY, watched apprehensively by DOT, rises and walks towards his bag)

MOLL: (watching HONEY stare down at his bag) Don't worry it won't run away, Mr. Honey. (she titters) - at least, I don't see any legs on it. Still, bags do give me the creeps. They're such nasty hide-aways, aren't they? Look at that ghastly Robert Montgomery in NIGHT MUST FALL.

TED: Who's he?

MOLL: For your information, mister ignorance, he was the star who played Danny who carried around the head of a woman in his bag. Or was it her other half? Anyway, they got him in the end.

TED: I should jolly well hope so.

MOLL: Course he was mad, you know, though you couldn't really tell until after he'd smothered poor old Dame May Whitty. Did you see the picture, Mr. Honey?

DOT: Moll, let's change the subject.

MOLL: Oh, Dot, don't be such an old priss. These things happen in life. Think of how many grizzly things get left in luggage rooms.

DOT: You've been seeing too many pictures, that's all.

MOLL: But you learn from the pictures, don't you, Mr. Honey?

                        (As HONEY fails to answer MOLL tenses)

                I said - you learn from the pictures, don't you,

Mr. Honey?

HONEY: (turning slowly) Do you... I mean... I don't see why not.

MOLL: Now you come and sit down here by me... come on.

(HONEY sits quietly on the sofa)

That's right. Now let me tell you about the time I saw Leslie Howard standing in the rain on Blackwater Station.

TED: Moll, what about getting us all a bit more coffee and cake?

MOLL: (to DOT) You do it, love, will you - I'm about all in. Drink doesn't agree with me, you know, seeing it doesn't

(She glares hard at ALF)

run in our family. Tell me, Mr. Honey, what do you think of drink?

(Sighing, DOT exits to kitchen. HONEY shrugs)

TED: Now come on, Molly, let him be.

MOLL: But he's got to talk - it's only polite.

(She nudges HONEY)

Isn't it?

(HONEY nods)

See, he does know his place. Now come on, Mr. Honey, I want your opinion.

HONEY: It has its uses.

MOLL: I beg your pardon, I didn't hear you.

TED: He said it had its uses, Moll, its uses.

MOLL: Of course from a man's point of view it would have.

TED: Just how do you mean?

MOLL: Women!

TED: (caressing MOLL gently on the back) Personally
speaking I hold no truck with drink if it's used for
that purpose, because I happen to like my women as
God made 'em - as straight and steady as a drink of
water.

MOLL: And as tasteless I suppose.

          (TED chuckles and ruffles her hair. She
          pushes away)

That's right, go and ruin ten and sixpence worth of
beautification - it's just what I would expect from
you.

TED: Now now, Moll.

MOLL: You wouldn't do a thing like that, would you, Mr.
Honey?

          (HONEY smiles)

See, Ted Ward.

HONEY: But I have.

MOLL: With a woman?

HONEY: Yes.

MOLL: You don't say.

          (She turns disbelieving eyes on TED who
          chuckles and pats HONEY on the back)

TED: Good for you, son.

MOLL: Well I think it's disgusting.

TED: Now come off it, Moll.

MOLL: Why is it that men have to boast so much. Always
talking about the women they've had and wronged -
it makes me sick. Really, if there's a dirtier word
than men I've yet to hear it.

TED: It can't be too bad, Moll - it's still only a three
letter word, you know.

MOLL: And let me tell you another thing, Ted Ward. Just
understand that what I've done in my life and where

I've been and who with has nothing whatsoever to do with you.

TED: But who said it had?   I'm not asking you for a case history, am I now?

MOLL: Oh yes you are. In your own sly way you're just dying to know all about the various men in my life just so you can stimulate yourself or lay down the law or something. Well, take it from me, mister nosy-parker, you're not going to know. He hasn't the right, has he, Mr. Honey?

HONEY: Not if it means raking in the ashes of the part.

MOLL: There, you see, Ted Ward.

TED: No, I don't see for maybe the past can rise like that myth bird they talk about. Maybe it's just as significant.

HONEY: But only if you believe in resurrections.

TED: Ay, and what if I do?

HONEY: Nothing.... for I suppose men must.

MOLL: But why must they?

HONEY: Because in the end it's the only hope they have. That way they can endure and go on bearing all that they suffer in this life by hoping... believing... that in the end... some intelligence....

TED: Why not say God?

HONEY: Because talk of a God implies worship. I used that other term to.... simplify.

TED: Are you trying to say that God is not God but something else?

HONEY: No, for God is indisputably God for those who believe in him. For the rest he's nothing if not a very dubious intelligence.

MOLL: For God's sake, how did we get onto God?

TED: Look, Mr. Honey, a lot of people talk like you - blaming God for this and that - for all their faults and deficiencies, but it's no criterion, damn it.

God's God and that's that and I'm plain tired of
listening to every little bright boy spout out his
venom against something he can't even hope to
understand unless.... he's...

(he hesitates)

HONEY: Unless he's what, Mr. Ward?

TED: Blamed if I know. I was going to say... suffered...
but then that's only a part of it. Man suffers but Man
also enjoys. It comes in turns, I guess... like the
toss of a coin.

HONEY: Does it, Mr. Ward? What happens then if it doesn't
come in turn, if a man has no luck. What then?

TED: It's not just a question of luck but of....

HONEY: Insight?

TED: No. Faith. And in my book that isn't so bad no
matter what the gamble is. It's a chance and in my
opinion that's all a man has the right to figure on.

HONEY: But then I am not a gambler, Mr. Ward.

TED: Then all I can say....

MOLL: What, don't tell me that you haven't tried the pools?

TED: Moll love, we're not talking about that kind of gambling.

MOLL: Well you don't have to be snotty about it. After all,
you're not the smartest thing in pants, you know.

ALF: (stirring in his sleep) What... what's that?

MOLL: Speak of the devil and you're sure to get his ammunition.

(ALF stretches and lets his hands fall
heavily onto his lap. Grunts)

TED: Poor old Alf. He's probably back at Passchendaele.

MOLL: Tell me, Mr. Honey, do you think it right that a
woman in her prime with a very young son, a small
boy....

TED: But Moll, Jim's fourteen!

MOLL: How do you know I was referring to Jim. Of all the
            cheek.....

TED: I thought you were, that's all.

MOLL: Oh be quiet. Mr. Honey, do you think it right that a
            woman should marry a man much older than herself?

TED: But he's no marriage counsellor, Moll.

MOLL: Will you please shut up and let the gentleman answer.

            (TED mutters and shakes his head)

            Well, Mr. Honey.

HONEY: There are young men whose minds are already
            fossilized and old men whose minds continue to burn
            and remain bright for all the days of their lives.

TED: Senator, now you're talking!

MOLL: But physically speaking. I mean - surely there's an
            enormous difference there?

HONEY: Are you thinking of children?

MOLL: Heavens no! I'm over that lark... I hope.

            (TED grins and fondles her shoulders. MOLL
            slaps his fingers)

            Behave yourself in front of company why can't you?

TED: But Mr. Honey's a man of the world: a quiet man
            who knows the facts of life - it wouldn't bother him.

MOLL: But you are, aren't you, Freddy?

            (HONEY smiles and shakes his head)

            Well never mind. Anyway, you are modest, you
            really are. In fact, I've made up my mind that you're
            a bit of a surprise package even if you are a bit....
            well... delicate. Still, that's not really important,
            is it? I mean... look at Robert Donat and Leslie
            Howard. What?

            (TED whispers in her ear and MOLL looks
            fretfully at HONEY)

What I wanted to say, Leslie, before I was so rudely interrupted is that I'm sorry about laughing like I did earlier on over Peter Lorre. I mean....

HONEY: Please, don't apologise - it's all finished with.

MOLL: Now that is sporting of you, really it is. It's just the way a gentleman would behave. Not like some others I happen to know.

TED: Moll, give over.

MOLL: Don't keep Molling me! As for you, you ought to apologise for that shaking you gave him - Frankenstein.

TED: By jove, you're right.

> (Thoughtfully he taps his chin, offers his hand)

Mr. Honey, I want you to accept this hand as a token of my esteem, as a gesture of friendship. I want you to take my hand......

MOLL: For Pete's sake give it to him before it withers away.

> (TED frowns but takes HONEY's hand and shakes it. HONEY withdraws his own hand quickly but TED doesn't seem to notice)

TED: There now, that's what I call a real white act: no recriminations, nothing but a big-hearted hand.

> (He chuckles)

You know, Mr. Honey, you and I and Alf and Hinds are going to make just one hell of a quartet.... do - ray - me - so!

MOLL: (laughing) Up the boys!

TED: That's the music.

> (He kisses MOLL)

By jove, what a night... what a winner of a night.... what a celebration!

> (He goes and claps ALF on the back)

Come on, wake up, Tommy Atkins.

ALF: All right, damn it, all right.

                        (TED and MOLL laugh.   ALF blinks and
                        glares around)

                Blast the lot of youse.

TED: (flinging an arm into the air)   Up the twenty-ninth!

                        (He begins to sing)

                Oh, we'll bung 'em in the earole and bung 'em in the
                        head
                And when we've bunged 'em everywhere....

ALF: We'll bung their lousy dead.
                Oh, we'll bung 'em in the brisket and bung 'em in the
                        rear....

TED & ALF: And when we've bunged 'em everywhere we'll give a
                rousing cheer.

ALF: Mons!

TED: Wipers!

ALF: The bloody Marne!

DOT: (rushing in from the kitchen)   What on earth....

                        (She gazes from one to the other)

ALF: (throwing up his arms)   It's war!

DOT: (pleasure softening her features)   How nice.

                        (As ALF and TED chuckle and whisper
                        together, HONEY stands and walks a few
                        paces towards his bag when MOLL calls)

MOLL: Mr. Honey.

                        (He stops - his back to her)

HONEY: Yes?

MOLL: (approaching and intimately taking his arm)   Now
                please excuse the question for we're all friends here,
                but are you ... married by any chance?

                        (HONEY shakes his head)

Then why aren't you? I mean... a man like you...
with your appearance so to speak?

HONEY: I suppose you could say.... because of my appearance.

MOLL: (laughs) Oh come off it. Now when I said that you
reminded me of Pat O'Brien I was quite wrong. In
fact, now that I think of it you remind me much
more of Lew Ayres when he used to play Dr. Kildare.
He was a quiet, serious, delicate sort of a man but
very good looking and quite popular with the ladies.

                    (ALF leans across and switches on the radio:
                    MUSIC UP - a soft, slow dance tune)

Though, mind you, I prefer Englishmen best - the
refined kind anyway. I'd do anything to meet Sir Larry
and that other nice fellow - Gregory something or
other. Dance?

                    (Taken completely by surprise, HONEY is
                    in her arms and MOLL hums to the tune.
                    As TED stands grinning, DOT goes to switch
                    off the radio but ALF grabs her arm)

ALF: No you don't - you leave it alone.

                    (As DOT stares at him, TED puts his hand
                    on her shoulder)

TED: Come on, Dottie, let's join the company.

DOT: Ted, I don't think.....

ALF: Go on and don't be a killjoy.

DOT: All right then.

                    (Not wanting to see MOLL with HONEY, she
                    rests her head on TED's chest while ALF
                    beats time to the music. They dance for a
                    minute or so when aroused, TED presses
                    DOT closely, murmuring in her ear. As
                    DOT makes to push TED away, he suddenly
                    bends forward and kisses her on the throat,
                    murmuring "Moll". DOT begins to laugh
                    as TED lets go of her to stare blankly about
                    him. Impulsed by DOT'S laughter, MOLL
                    suddenly reaches up and kisses HONEY on
                    the mouth. With a small cry he wrenches
                    away from her and stands bleakly shaking

his head. The music ends abruptly and
ALF switches off the wireless)

MOLL: (to HONEY) Why, you rotten little fairy.

(She moves to claw him)

DOT: Moll! Don't!

(As MOLL hesitates, TED grabs her hands)

TED: Now take it easy, Moll, take it easy. (to HONEY)
You better get out of here, son - quick!

(HONEY nods)

MOLL: Oh no he doesn't. I want to know why he did that to
me - why, I've never been so insulted in all my life.

ALF: (thumping the armrests) And neither have I!

TED: Hold it, Alf!

ALF: Damned if I will.

TED: Look Alf, I know what I'm doing.

ALF: Then you'd better let me in on it because I don't and
as this is my house I'm going to see that the likes of
him over there don't try to turn it into a pig sty.

DOT: (leaning wearily against the sideboard) Alf, you're
talking nonsense.

ALF: Quiet you - you're in this up to your neck.

(DOT laughs in the same bitter way as before.
MOLL shakes her)

MOLL: Now stop it, stop it!

(As DOT begins to sob quietly in her hands
MOLL puts a protective arm around her)

Don't, honey, don't go and make a spectacle of
yourself.... they're not worth it.

(She faces HONEY angrily)

You're responsible for this.

ALF: As I could have told you.

TED: Well, Mr. Honey?

                    (HONEY shakes his head)

           Well, you'd better do some thinking about it, senator,
           because it seems to me that the cards are stacked
           against you. Now if I were you I'd humbly apologise
           to the company......

ALF: Will somebody here please tell me why we are
           proceeding with this rigmarole?

TED: What would you have us do - hang him first?

MOLL: For Pete's sake, Ted, get on with it and ignore the
           public gallery.

ALF: Now you listen to me....

TED: No!

                    (Frustrated, ALF tries to rise but finding
                    it too difficult sits back with a groan)

           Now, Mr. Honey, would you mind telling us why you
           came here in the first place?

HONEY: There was a room vacant.

TED: That doesn't answer my question. There are thousands
           of rooms plastered all over this town and yet you had to
           come here. People usually have a good reason for
           wanting a particular room. What's yours?

HONEY: I had no reason. I simply wanted a place to rest in.

MOLL: (throwing back her head and laughing) Why, I never
           heard such muck in all my life. Little boy blue came
           blowing his horn at 19 Brewer Street to find rest and
           silence. He's a liar!

TED: Easy now, Moll.

MOLL: Oh shut up.

ALF: As the land lord of this establishment I do know that
           this gentleman entered my premises and practically
           bogged in them - like a bloody Hindu. I saw him on
           the make for Moll just as soon as he saw that you

were an old man, Ted, and I a chaired cripple.

TED: I'm sorry, Alf, but I can't believe that.

ALF: Oh, so I'm a liar, am I?

TED: It doesn't ring true and you know it.

MOLL: Go on then, mister prosecutor, and butter him up for a kiss why don't you.... why, you might do better than me.

> (She laughs as TED, grimmer now, faces HONEY)

TED: Well, you heard them, son, so what do you say?

> (Silence)

Answer me.

> (Silence)

All right then, take your time... take your time, but sooner than later you're going to have to answer me. Now what do you say?

> (Silence)

Answer me, damn it!

> (Silence. Gritting his teeth, TED takes HONEY by the collar and begins to shake him violently)

Now answer me, do you hear me, answer me!

DOT: Ted... don't!

> (Dazedly, TED relaxes his grip and stares about him)

ALF: Gawd, man, you nearly throttled him.

TED: (dropping his hands heavily to his sides he faces each one in turn)   He... he... wouldn't answer me.

MOLL: What did you expect?

TED: An answer... just an answer.

ALF: By half throttling him? That's not the way, Ted, we do it over here.

TED: What the hell do you mean?

ALF: What I said. Might be all right over there what with their lynch mobs and all but you ought to remember first and foremost that you were once an Englishman.

TED: So I was, godamnit, but not one of your bigot breed, Alf Lister!

MOLL: That's right - scream and wake the dead.

TED: (pointing to HONEY) Then try it!

ALF: But then you nearly throttled him.

TED: At your instigation.

MOLL: Oh stop it.

        (She goes between the two men)

        Remember that we're .... we're... not the only ones here. There's a poor sick boy upstairs probably frightened half to death, what with him having to listen to you.

        (She gives a sob and covers her face with her hands. TED places a soft hand on her shoulder)

TED: Molly love, Mollywog... my old Mollykins.

MOLL: (shaking off his hand) You make me sick.

TED: Moll, I didn't mean it, love, I didn't mean it.

MOLL: That's what I thought. Alan Ladd would have.

TED: Who?

MOLL: What's it matter except to know that he wouldn't have acted like you.

TED: How do you mean?

ALF: (in a loud and grilling whisper) Why, you nearly throttled him.

TED: (nodding and putting his hands in his pockets) In that case then - mister prosecutor withdraws.

        (he faces HONEY)

There's not a thing in the world to keep you here now, son - you can go.

        (As HONEY looks into his face TED turns away, his head bowed. MOLL stiffles a scream)

MOLL: You're a coward, Ted Ward!

TED: (turning to her) Oh no I'm not and I've never been. I've fought the best, my girl, and fought fair... in the ring, in court, and in every unholy kind of establishment known to mankind.   The verdict's always been that I fought fair - and I will again.

MOLL: That's why you half choked him, I suppose... why you shook him out like a rug until his teeth rattled. I know all about you and your fairness. You'd belt a woman and kick a dog as soon as look at them.

TED: You're wrong, Moll... wrong. All I was trying to do was make the man answer.

ALF: By throttling him?

        (Clenching and unclenching his hands, TED stares ahead)

TED: A long time ago something like this happened to me. Maybe it was in Butte, Montana - maybe not but nonetheless... it happened. I'd picked up a coloured boy for something or other and put him behind bars and that same night some of the honourable and enterprising citizens of that town wanted him out. I fought fair that day and they didn't get him. Sunday I was in church right in the front pew when the good reverend Sloe finished his sermon by spitting in my eye.   Holy of holies, he said, may the motes now melt and everafter, brother, see you white.

        (pause as they withdraw into themselves)

DOT: (gazing at HONEY) If anyone hurts one hair of his head you'll all pay for it.

                    (All but HONEY turn to stare at her)

          Yes, you'll pay for it... every one of you. He's not,
          you see, what you think he is.

TED: Then you tell us, Dottie, who and what he is?

MOLL: How would she know. I'll tell you what he is.

                    (Gliding towards HONEY she holds out her
                    hands to him.)

          Now... lill dollboy dance for mumsy Moll.... lill
          dollboy dance...

                    (She throws her arms about him and begins
                    to sway)

TED: Moll, leave him alone.

ALF: No, go ahead, Moll, and show us what he is.

                    (DOT puts her head in her hands as MOLL
                    swings HONEY around then quickly steps
                    away from him. MOLL and ALF laugh as
                    TED steps in and stops him from falling)

TED: Are you all right, son?

HONEY: Water.

MOLL: What's lill dollboy want?

TED: He wants some water.

ALF: Then get him some and let him and Moll do it again.

TED: No. Just give him the shove and be done with him.

ALF: What are you afraid of, Ted?

TED: It isn't decent.

MOLL: Old methodist.

TED: I believe in God if that's what you mean.

ALF: And here I was thinking you believed in the United
          States.

TED: Ay, and so I do.

            (ALF chuckles and slaps his game leg)

HONEY: Water.

MOLL: Watch little boy blue for me will you while I go and
            get him something to drink.

TED: Yes, you do that, Moll.

            (MOLL goes out to the kitchen as TED
            slowly walks around HONEY who stands
            quite still)

            You know, I might be wrong, but I wouldn't be
            surprised if our friend here took dope.

ALF: Neither would I by the looks of him.

TED: Mind you, it's hard to tell unless you examine them
            properly, but at least he has the looks of a man who
            carries the monkey on his back.

            (He stands in front of HONEY and looks him
            in the eye)

            Maybe if you could speak, senator, you'd tell us all
            to go to hell and maybe I'd even agree with you, but
            now's the time I think you told us who you are.

ALF: He's a flipping Mr. Coffey or someone - that's all he
            is.

TED: Somewhere along the line I'll find out because it
            doesn't make sense, Alf, it doesn't make sense.
            All he claims he wants is peace and rest and yet he's
            clung to us like a leech. Why, is what I want to know.
            Why didn't he beg off before and clear out upstairs?
            Is it because he's afraid of being alone, afraid that if
            he's left to himself he'll give himself away?

            (TED scratches his skull)

            Or could it be, Alf, that he doesn't care a damn what
            actually happens to himself?

ALF: He cares all right otherwise why would he ask for a
            room in the first place?

TED: Maybe because he's on the run.

ALF: Na-ow.

TED: And why not?

ALF: Instinct. This bloke hasn't run off from anything or
            anybody unless he's a sky pilot run off from his
            bishop.

                    (He chuckles saltily - alone)

            Fact is, I'd bet my bottom dollar that he's just been
            let out of a loony bin.

TED: Or a monastery?

ALF: Or Rookwood cemetery or that open jail they've got
            for perverts.

HONEY: Water.

TED: The poor bastard's just asked for water.

ALF: Damn it, I ought to charge him for all the drink he's
            drunk.

TED: The hell you say. Most of it was mine.

ALF: So it was now, so it was. Now blast this leg o' mine.

TED: Take it easy, Alf.

ALF: Take it easy, he says, take it easy. Why should I
            take it easy. It's not your pain, is it?

TED: I told you before... you ought to have it off. Cork,
            they say, makes a pretty good substitute.

ALF: Does it now, and since when may I ask have you
            become an expert on flaming cork legs?

TED: Forget it, Alf. Dottie's over there looking like
            death warmed up.

ALF: (turning to DOT) Eh you, snap out of it!

                    (DOT shakes her head)

TED: What is it, Dottie?

DOT: I know what he is now.

(ALF groans)

TED: What, Dottie?

DOT: I can't tell you. You would only laugh at him.

TED: Look, I'm your friend, Dottie. You can tell me and I'll promise you I won't laugh at him. Now what is he?

DOT: (staring at HONEY with an expression of reverence) He's... he's... the new share.

         (ALF groans and TED gives a deprecatory shrug as MOLL enters from kitchen - a glass of liquid held close to her breast)

ALF: Ah, Gunga Din at last.

MOLL: Mind your business.

         (Smiling, she raises the glass to HONEY'S lips; he drinks. MOLL begins to giggle)

Now that... that beats the band... beats anything I ever saw. It even beats Spencer Tracy as Dr. Jekyll anyday!

TED: What's so funny, Moll?

MOLL: (pointing at HONEY)   Him.

TED: Well, what's so funny about him?

MOLL: Well, he drank it.

ALF: And why shouldn't he... it was on the house, wasn't it?

MOLL: Yes, but....

         (She giggles infectiously)

TED: But what?

MOLL: Well... it was vinegar.

         (DOT draws a sharp breath and holds her head. Pause as ALF and TED stare at her)

TED: Moll love, why did you... have to go... and do a thing like that for?

MOLL: Dunno. Dunno exactly. Unless... well you know... to pay him back for that kiss I expect. Teach him... sort of... you know... not to take liberties. It was only a bit of vinegar anyway.

(DOT gasps)

ALF: (turning on her) Now you cut that nonsense out!

TED: (shaking his head) What the hell's got into us?

MOLL: But it didn't seem to hurt him, did it? I mean (giggles) it'll only pickle his tongue a bit, won't it... sort of... preserve it like... till the next time. But the strange thing is... he didn't even flinch!

TED: (shaking his head) Molly.... Moll.

(He goes and takes her in his arms as she buries her head on his chest. Disdainfully ALF frames a silent "bah" and drops his head on his chest)

HONEY: Water!

(Silently DOT goes to him and looks him in the eyes. Taking up one of his hands she puts it to her lips. Raising her head, MOLL stares unbelievingly at her)

MOLL: Dot! Dot!

(Pulling away from TED she takes DOT by the shoulders)

For Pete's sake, Dot, what do you think you're doing?

DOT: Nothing... nothing.

MOLL: Nothing! Ted... did you see what she was doing? She was kissing his hand!

(She shakes DOT who is almost in a stupor)

Wake up, Dot, wake up! Ted, don't stand there like a hatrack - do something!

HONEY: Water.

(DOT pulls away from MOLL)

DOT: Just look what you've all gone and done to him. Look what you've gone and done to him and he.... him.... a saint!

ALF: (jerking to wakefulness) What's that, what's that?

DOT: Yes, a saint, a saint!

(As MOLL slaps her across the cheek, HONEY cries out and sinks to his knees as the curtain falls)

CURTAIN

ACT THREE

SCENE: The Living room.

TIME: Half an hour later.

(As the CURTAIN RISES, HONEY is stretched
out on the sofa, a blanket over him. With
his head down, ALF dozes in his chair.
TED is slowly pacing the room. Finally
he stops short of the sofa and looks down at
HONEY)

TED: Now what is a man, God tell me, what is a man to
act like that... to faint away at the drop of a hat?
Or... what isn't a man. Isn't. What does a man
lack to have to do a thing like that? Is it because he
doesn't pray, doesn't believe, doesn't give a damn
for anything? And even if he doesn't what right has
that man to inflict himself on others and so make
them care instead? Or is the answer in the fact that
he's sick and dying from the inside out?

(He shakes his head slowly)

Yet the question remains... what is the nature of that
man? What kind of a poor lost pilgrim is he to have
turned up here for peace and quiet? I meant well,
damn it, I meant well and if he had talked....?

(He shakes his head)

And yet... the question is... what kind of man am I?

(He frowns and raising a finger points it at
ALF)

Alf, can you hear me?

(Silence)

Alf!

(Silence)

All the same, Alf, you're going to be my witness. I
want you to know that I'm a man of pride and proud
of it. I'm not ashamed, you understand, not ashamed.

(Pause)

I've done things. I've used myself, godamnit...
gone out into the world and met it... met it, you
understand?

> (Pause as he listens a moment then lowers
> his voice)

It's all writ large in the Book of Man... it's there all
right. I don't have to lie to nobody... nobody, you
understand?

> (Pause)

All right then, so go ahead and remind me that a
man fails and gets hurt and come to realise in the
stoppage of his growth that he isn't the man he thought
he was. Just tell me that and I'll buy it. I'll buy it
because I know it!

> (Pause)

But that don't mean to say that a man hasn't the right
to his pride in knowing that what he did right he
might even have done better had not the whole crazy
world conspired against him just to make him assume
the average size. But no matter - I'll buy that too.
I buy it because I know it!

> (Pause)

Yet that doesn't mean to say that a man has to kid
himself that he wasn't any better than another. I
was, by God, and I knew it... know it!

> (As he pauses MOLL enters from the hall
> door. She is wearing over her dress a
> smart black spring coat)

MOLL: Were you and Saint Honey having one of your little
cozy chats?

TED: You can see that he's sleeping.

MOLL: Then who were you talking to... your better half?

TED: Alf.

MOLL: By the looks of him you must have bored him to
death.

TED: For Chris' sake!

MOLL: Don't swear at me - I'm tired of it. A man of your age ought to have learned by now how to treat a woman, but oh no... you still think she's some sort of fixture you can hang your spleen on whenever you like, but you're wrong, dear. In fact you're so wrong it makes me sick just to think about it.

TED: Why do we have to squabble like this? Isn't there enough hell in the world without you and I adding to it? Why don't we just clear out and honeymoon someplace - in the Cotswolds or in Scotland, and then after a fort-night.....

MOLL: A fort-night!

TED: What's wrong with that?

MOLL: At ten and six a night I suppose to go with it. Oh no, Mister Everready, you'll have to do a little better than that if you expect to use my laundry basket.

TED: (catching hold of her wrists) Now Moll love, listen to me, will you, listen for a moment.

(MOLL gives a half-articulated cry and tries to free herself)

MOLL: Dot! Dot!

TED: Please Moll, listen, will you?

(As TED tries to pull her closer, MOLL unexpectedly slips to her knees. TED watches registering deep concern as she slowly gets to her feet. Tentatively he puts an arm about her)

Molly, love, my old Mollykins.

(As he squeezes her she cries out and he lets go of her)

MOLL: Why do you have to be so clumsy... you hurt me then!

TED: I didn't mean to, Moll... you know that. Earlier on tonight when I grabbed you in the hall... you didn't seem to mind. You... you... kissed me back.

MOLL: I know.

TED: Well, it was a great moment, wasn't it?

> (MOLL glances down, TED takes a pace or
> two, stops and swivels - bangs a fist into
> his palm)

Well it was for me anyway. It was as though I was
being born again... do you know that? Me? Born
again! I felt young and strong and clean and yet at
the same time I felt shame.

> (Silence as he shakes his head and stares
> ahead)

Shame if you want to know for not having done what I
should have done years ago. Shame for kidding myself
over the years that I never needed a wife or son.
Shame even in thinking that I was unworthy of them.
Even shame in thinking that it mightn't be too late to
start.

> (MOLL has lowered her head and seems to
> be examining one of her stockings near the
> knee)

You'll never know just what a precious moment it was
even though I kept telling myself that I was being
sentimental and that sentimentality wasn't sense
and yet underneath I knew... that I loved you, Moll.

> (MOLL raises her head and glares at TED
> with contempt)

MOLL: You bastard you... look what you made me do!

> (She points to her knee where a hole has
> appeared in her stocking)

My God, fifteen bob... fifteen bloody bob chucked
down the drink and for what... for what... will you
tell me that?

TED: I'm sorry, Moll.

MOLL: Of course you're sorry! All the same you just wanted
to give me a gentle little maul like you did to Saint
Honey there, didn't you? Well, you're not going to
get the chance again, sweetheart. I'm going to meet
a man who'll really take care of me - and my stockings!

TED: And if you think I'm going to stand idly by while you run off to meet some Tom, Dick, or Harry, you're mistaken.

MOLL: Tom, Dick, or Harry nothing. His name's Bill, dear: Mr William Hitchens of the Main Roads Board. And though he doesn't earn fifteen pounds a week he's big and young and gentle with a woman - the William Holden type if you want to know.

          (She laughs)

     Still, I don't see why you and I can't remain friends or would you prefer me to be a sister to you?

TED: All I planned was for you and I to be together... to get along... the three of us... you and I and the boy. And what I said awhile back still goes. I want to take care of you and Jim.

MOLL: Oh come off it. For the past half hour or so you've done nothing but dote on that psycho there while I've been alone upstairs.

TED: The man passed out, Moll. He needed help.

MOLL: And so did I but you were too busy holding onto his little frozen hand.

TED: Moll love, don't be like that.

MOLL: Don't Moll me again, Ted, I'm tired of it do you hear, tired of it.

TED: And we were going to be married.

MOLL: (inspecting her left hand) Were we? But then I haven't anything to show for it, have I now? In fact if I were you I'd think about marrying Saint Honey instead - he'd be so obliging, I'm sure. Just think of all the little vows you could bring into the world.

          (As she laughs TED takes a menacing step towards her)

     That's right, hit me why don't you... you great twitching lump of age!

          (TED slowly turns his back on her)

TED: (softly) Where's Dot?

MOLL: Being sick or powdering her nose... so just leave her alone. Now I'm getting out of here so good-night mister Everready.

(Silence)

I said good-night.

(Silence)

Then go to hell.

(MOLL slams the hall door after her which awakens ALF who sits up and blinks about him)

ALF: I had the most terrible dream, you know. I was trapped in some sort of a pit when this old leg o' mine gave out and frightened the hell out of me. I couldn't move it see... it was like dragging a chain about... a big chain... one of those big ship chains... you know... one of those big liner chains.

(He shakes his head)

Anyway, what have you been up to?

TED: Minding my own business.

ALF: Oh, you have, have you? That's very interesting, isn't it? Tell me, what's come over you?

TED: Nothing.

ALF: (waving his arms about as he sings) Oh we'll bung 'em in the nothing and bung 'em in the ruts
And when we've bunged 'em nowhere we'll bung their lousy nuts...
We'll bung 'em in the spokeshave and bung 'em in... the...

(He chuckles and looks around: sees HONEY stretched out)

Hullo, now don't tell me... let me guess... he's died.

(TED grunts)

Well I'll tell you one thing. If he's passed out here I'll sell him to the Jews.

(TED grunts)

I'll sell him to the Jews all right in order to pay the ground rent for the way he flops all over my place. Oh, he's a flopper all right, isn't he? Just think of the trouble we would have had if he'd been female.

(He chuckles lewdly)

I'd have had this place chalked up as a knocking shop. Alfred Lister's home for fainting floppers and the house specialty - Saints at a guinea a throw.

(TED grunts followed by a pause)

You know, I ought to charge him for that blanket.

TED: He's had it like the rest of us - tired and worn out with living. I tell you the whole damned world's tired.

ALF: Not me. Except for this poor old leg o' mine I'm as good a man as ever I was, and as for him... he's still a chicken in comparison and yet look at him. I've seen corpses look healthier.

TED: Corpses have nothing to worry about and that man has. It sticks out a mile. But then, there's something wrong with all of us.

ALF: Now wait a tick, Ted - that doesn't sound like you.

TED: You spend your life waiting and for what - a coronary thrombosis, peace, a pension, a wife, the old folks home and the grave. Life's full of waiting and I'm tired of it.

ALF: You talk as if someone's shaken you up a bit?

TED: So what... I'm seventy three.

ALF: Yet only an hour ago you were gallivanting about like a young buck of twenty.

TED: Then poor fool me. I ought to have known better. I ought to have damned well known better.

ALF: Well of course you could be right in taking that point of view because, well, just between you and me now, I don't think at your age, mind you, that er... you could have kept up with Moll if you know what I mean.

TED: (nodding)   How right you are.

ALF: Now don't go jumping to conclusions. I didn't mean to imply that you were too old or anything like that. I simply meant.....

TED: Forget it. Moll's of a different generation.

           (He stares at his knuckles)

ALF: But in the long run that doesn't mean a thing with a woman. Why, Moll's pushing forty one.

TED: And I'm seventy three.

ALF: But it's different with a woman. In a couple of years she will have had it and come running at the wink of an eye. They're long in the tooth by then, you know, and the menopause you might say is the kiss of death.

           (He glances about)

      Why, just take a look at Dot.

TED: The fact remains that Moll is of a different generation and one that I don't particularly care about.

           (He shakes his head and mumbles)

      Why, the bastards don't even fight fair.

ALF: What... what's that?

TED: Nothing. I said I'm thinking of pulling out. Go down to Blackwater and live with my sister Amy. After all, she's only seventy five.

ALF: But heavens man, she's as deaf as a post and calls you mister Chambers! Why, you wouldn't be able to talk to her and what good is that to a man who loves his chat over a pint?

TED: She's flesh and blood, Alf, and might have need of me and that's reason enough. For instance, I could remind her of the old folks and what we did as kids. She'd remember.

ALF: And probably blame you for it. I can just see her - an old toothless frump sitting up like a wax doll in a nightshirt.

TED: Alf, I'll have you know that you're talking about my sister Amy.

ALF: All right then, all right, so it's your blooming funeral.

TED: Ay, and it might well be but no matter. A time comes when a man's got to come to terms with his years.

ALF: But you're not aged, man, you're not aged!

TED: We're a passing generation, Alf.

ALF: But that has nothing to do with it. It's the way you feel that counts... the way you look at things. O'Keefe only said to me the other day when I hobbled down for that drink... he said to me, Mister Lister, that Ted Ward's the best preserved man for his years that I've ever had the pleasure to look on and you know what I told him? I said... look here O'Keefe... oh yes, O'Keefe I called him. I said - O'Keefe - you cut that age business out or Mr. Ward will be down himself to cut up that mug of yours. I said... O'Keefe, you just listen to me and he did, you know with that soppy Irish look of his. I said - that man's fit and young enough to knock you and yours back across the channel, O'Keefe, and don't you forget it. I tell you, Ted, he was so impressed that he unwittingly knocked off a couple of bob.

TED: I still say we're a passing generation.

ALF: Ted... look. Take the war for instance.

TED: Alf, let's put R.I.P. over the war - all wars, shall we? Let's not bull ourselves into believing that they meant a damned thing to anyone.

ALF: It did to me.

TED: Ay, I know that but that's not quite the same thing. You need a war like some men need a woman. Without one you'd have nothing to hang your manhood on.

ALF: You're... you're having... a go at me.

TED: Then you're reading me wrong. I'm not having a go at you anymore than I am at that poor drifter there.

(He indicates HONEY)

Looks peaceful, doesn't he, and yet I'll bet he's full of turmoil... full of fear and worry... full of something anyway.   But then...who am I to know?

(He stands and stretches himself)

ALF: It took everything away from me that war.   I was a right good centre half, you know.   Ackrington Stanley wanted me and so did Stoke and I would have gone only that girl Maggie let me down and married that Rugby bloke from Hull and finished up, you know, selling it on the Bayswater Road.   And then I got plastered that day and got sucked in by those drums and that one-armed bloke screaming his nelly off about the glory of the British Army and before I knew it I was Plummer's runner there in Flanders.   Send for Lister he'd say... he's got the best pair of legs in the Corps.   I did too... damned good pins they were. I was built strong in the thigh, you know, and I had a pair of calves you couldn't throw a rope around.   And yet look at me now.   This... this... poor old leg o' mine.....

TED: Give it a rub.

ALF: I can't.

TED: Yes you can.

ALF: I can't I tell you.

TED: Then give in to it and call it a day.

ALF: That's a fine way to talk, isn't it now - call it a day, he says, call it a day as if I were ready for the knackers.   Well I aren't, my boy, you mark my words.

TED: Night, Alf.

ALF: Aren't you going to stop for a nightcap or something?

(TED is shaking his head when DOT enters from the hall)

DOT: How is he now, Ted?

(She moves towards HONEY)

TED: I guess he's still asleep, Dottie.   He'll be all right.

ALF: Now don't go touching him for Chris' sake - just
            leave him alone.

                    (Satisfied that HONEY is all right she faces
                     the two men)

DOT: Where's Moll?

TED: She went out, Dottie.

DOT: Then why aren't you with her?

TED: Dottie, Moll's an awful self-reliant woman. She
            doesn't need me anymore than she needs that...
            gentleman there.

                    (He points at HONEY)

ALF: There you go again thinking that you're aged.

DOT: But Ted, I don't understand.   What do you mean when
            you say that she doesn't need you anymore. You're
            engaged to her, aren't you?   What does she mean by
            running off like this?

ALF: Ever since that husband of hers died she's had an
            itch in her drawers.

TED: (appealing to ALF)   Alf.....

DOT: Ted, I am asking you a question.

TED: Well, what do you want me to say - that I sent her
            out on a message or something?   Well I didn't.
            Where she's gone to is her own business and she
            doesn't have to account for it to you or me or to
            anyone else.

DOT: But I thought she'd be here with you. I had no idea
            she was going out.   I thought she'd got over it.   I
            mean... she said... she's gone to meet that Hitchens
            fellow, hasn't she?

TED: Dot, I don't know. If she has it's her own ... funeral.
            I'm finished caring now.   I'm tired and want to go to
            bed.

ALF: That Moll's going to finish up on the Bayswater Road
            if she's not careful.

DOT: She's run out on you, hasn't she, Ted?

TED: Don't blame her, Dottie.   After all, Moll's young and still attractive and what with that sick boy up there she needs a break.   And I'm... well I'm seventy three, you know, and it's no use me pretending that I understand the younger generation.

DOT: But Jim thinks the world of you.

TED: And I'll see that the boy's looked after, don't you worry.   But Moll, you know, well, she has her interests and I have mine.   I don't know anything about films and actors and people like that and she actually thought that Dempsey, mind you, was an Irish comedian.

                    (He chuckles to himself)

          Well, no matter now.   Everyone, I say, to his own... christmas pudding.

                    (He starts to walk to the hall door when two sharp raps sound on it.   He frowns and slowly turns.   DOT goes and gently takes him by the arm)

DOT: Come and sit down, Ted, and have a cup of something. She'll get over it, you'll see.   Now come on.

TED: All right, Dottie, but it goes against the grain.

DOT: Thank you, Ted.

                    (The raps sound again)

ALF: Will somebody mind opening the door!

DOT: (nervously)   Come in.

                    (The door opens and HINDS and ENID enter the living room.   There is a brashness about HINDS but he is also nervous and the girl obviously so.   Her dress is neat but somehow 'wrong')

          Oh... it's you, Mr. Hinds.

          (HINDS nods and pushes ENID forward)

HIND: May I present Enid... Enid Barlowe.

          (The girl tries to muster a smile but it

collapses into a sniffle. HINDS pinches her
arm)

Pack it in, Enid.

(TED takes out a pocket handkerchief and
offers it to her)

TED: Here, young lady, take this.

(She shakes her head and takes HINDS'
handkerchief from his breast pocket and
puts it to her nose)

DOT: (touching the girl's elbow) Now come on in dear,
and make yourself at home. You too, Mr. Hinds.

(HINDS nods at her but it is ALF who has his
attention)

HINDS: It's like this, Mr. Lister. Enid and I went to the
registry office this afternoon to see about getting
married but there was a hitch and we have to go back
tomorrow. Meanwhile Enid here had to clear out
from home and so can't go back and we thought we
could share my room seeing it's vacant, seeing that
Pat went yesterday.

ALF: And she's not Irish?

(HINDS looks blank)

I said.... is she Irish?

DOT: Alf, you've no right to get personal that way.

ALF: If I've told you once I've told you a hundred times. I
will not have another Irish creature in my house....
now is that clear?

DOT: Alf!

HINDS: Enid was born and bred here... all her life.

ALF: That's all I wanted to know.

DOT: But Mr. Hinds, where have you been all this time?

HINDS: To the Odeon. Enid wanted to see the picture there.

TED: (shaking his head) The new generation.

HINDS: It will be all right, won't it - the room and all?

ALF: Of course it will, Harry, of course it will. However, there's just one thing.

         (HINDS looks blank)

         I said, Harry... there's just one thing.

DOT: Alf, don't shout.

ALF: I've got to if his machine's turned off.

         (HINDS checks his hearing air - a breast pocket affair. It makes a static sound then is silent)

HINDS: I can hear clear enough.

ALF: Good.   First of all before you settle down for a trial run....

DOT: Alf, don't talk like that.

ALF: What's wrong with you - it's only a joke, isn't it? Everybody these days does what we should have done, my girl.   Prove before you buy.   All I want to say is that before Harry and his young bride-to-be settle down for the night I want him to give this old leg o' mine a rub.

HINDS: You hear that Enid... we're in!

DOT: But Alf, what about Mr. Honey?

         (Pause as all stare at the man on the sofa)

HINDS: Enid, stop that sniffling, will you. Who's he?

ALF: (pointing)   That's what we'd all like to know. But that's him - wearing out the sofa you might say. Does nothing but go on the nod or faint away like a... like a twopenny saint!   And I've had it, I tell you, I've had it.

DOT: But he can't go, Alf.   He's paid.

ALF: Be hanged if he won't and will.

DOT: But Alf.....

ALF: Do you think, woman, that I'd let... think of...
letting this young couple... this pair of decent kids
bust up a happy union on account of that article over
there? Do you imagine for one minute that I'd let
them whimper about the town at this ungodly hour in
search of a bed because Alfred J. hard-hearted
Lister chucked the book at them? Do you? Good
heavens, woman, what can you be thinking of?

DOT: Mr. Honey.

ALF: Ah-r-r-r!

TED: Listen to me, Alf.

ALF: You heard what she said... thinking of Mister Honey
so she says. I know what she's thinking all right.
Well get it out of your mind do you hear me, get it
out of your mind!

TED: Must I shout to be heard!

(TED glares hard at ALF who in turn glares
hard at the sniffling girl)

ALF: Harry, for Chris' sake, tell her to put the plug in,
will you?

HINDS: Blow your nose, Enid.

(She does so as TED clears his throat and
takes up a position near ALF)

ALF: Thinking of mister Honey so she says. I know what
she means all right, don't think I don't. Well it won't
happen in my house, let me tell you that. You can do
your dirty business somewhere else... you can clear
out but you're not going to turn this place into a pig
sty... not while I'm alive and not when I'm dead
either. I'll sell up this place over your head before
that happens, you see if I don't.

TED: Do I get to say my piece or don't I?

ALF: Thinking of Mr. Honey indeed.

TED: Either I get to say my piece or I leave this room
never to return.

ALF: Ted, there's something going on here behind my back
and I want to know about it.

DOT: It's all in your head, Alf - your anger, your persecutions, your suspicions.....

ALF: Suspicions is right but don't worry - I'll get the facts to put you back in the gutter.

DOT: That's right... put me back where you found me - at the head of a bunch of snotty kids. Dottie Warboys - good sister, big sister, poor old workhorse. The girl who was stupid enough to come in out of the rain - who fell for the oldest gag in the world - security. Well it doesn't matter anymore, Alf, you see. It doesn't matter.

ALF: No? Well we'll see about that. We'll see about that when you're down on your uppers - a ten bob touch for any drunk or black.

TED: Damn it, that's enough!

ALF: Now wait a tick, whose side do you think you're on?

TED: I said I was tired of waiting and I didn't lie.

(Silence but for ENID'S sniffling)

No one need leave this house. No one. To-night Mr. Honey can stay where he is and tomorrow you can move him into my room. I'm off as I said to my sister Amy's.

DOT: Oh Ted, you never said a word to me.

TED: I know, Dottie, I know, but Amy needs me. Only awhile ago she said to me... Mister Chambers, I'm a lonely old woman she said... no one cares for me. Cried she did. Broke me up. She was a good girl, Amy - a great knitter. The least we can do now is to comfort one another.

ALF: But that's no compensation if she's as deaf as a post - pardon me, Harry - and calls you Mister Chambers!

TED: Alf, I'll have you know you're referring to my sister Amy.

ALF: That's right - a stranger!

DOT: But it's his sister.

ALF: A batty old woman who knows next to nothing about the man, her own brother mind you, who fought the greatest heavyweight the world has ever seen. A man furthermore who's done things, been things, seen things, who's even killed a man. And what about our Moll, eh, what about her?

TED: I told you before, Alf. We're of different generations.

ALF: Do you mean to stand there and tell me that you're not going to marry that poor girl?

TED: God's will be done, Alf.

(Stupified, ALF leans back in his chair and there is a pause. ENID sniffles)

HINDS: If you don't mind Enid and I will find somewhere else, thank you, won't we, Enid?

ENID: Yes.... I want to go home.

DOT: That's silly talk, dear. We'll make some arrangement, don't you worry.

ALF: (pointing) All we've got to do is to get rid of that man there!

TED: He's paid and he's waited and so you're obliged to let him stay.

ALF: Obliged nothing... not while I'm master of this house.

DOT: Alf, why rankle this way?

ALF: Because I've eyes in my head, that's why. Because I've been blest with the gift of seeing how a man is put together, that's why. Because I'm a judge of character and know when to call a shovel a bloody spade. You call that rankling? Well I call it sanity and belive me, woman, I'm sticking by the sane.

HINDS: If it's all the same to you, Enid and I can doss in the park, can't we, Enid?

ENID: Yes, but I want to go home.

ALF: You just stay where you are, Harry, and comfort that poor child. If anyone's going it's him!

(He points at HONEY)

DOT: No one's going.

ALF: Then we'll see about that.

            (With surprising agility he bends and picks
            up an empty glass. As he aims it at
            HONEY TED comes and stands in his line
            of flight. As they dodge about a bit ALF
            finally and hopelessly throws the glass against
            the wall)

Damn you, Ward, damn you!

DOT: Alf.... please.

ALF: So that's how it is, is it - a couple of cuckoos in the
            nest, is it? Well, we'll see about that, you see if
            we don't. I don't want to see either of you again...
            you can both clear out.

TED: You go on like this, Alf, and you'll never make the
            Book of Man.

ALF: You and your scriptures and fake honesty. I've had
            enough of you. Go ahead and coddle that old sow in
            Blackwater why don't you and get her to knit you a
            muffler. Harry!

            (HINDS' head shoots up)

You take that girl of yours and get upstairs, do you
hear me. The room's yours.

DOT: If you don't mind, please stay where you are, Mr.
            Hinds.

            (HINDS glances from DOT to ALF assessing
            who has the advantage)

ALF: Harry, do as I say... get upstairs!

            (As ENID squeals HINDS grabs her by the
            hand and bolts outside - banging the door)

            (Pause)

DOT: (wearily) All right, Alf.... so you got your way.

            (She glances sadly at HONEY)

ALF: Now go on... wake him up.

TED: Hold it, Alf.

ALF: Either she wakes him up or I do it myself.

> (He begins to rise from his chair as DOT moves to him)

DOT: Alf, please.....

ALF: Wake him, I tell you.

DOT: No!

> (As she moves closer to him, ALF pushes her in the chest and sends her reeling)

TED: That's done it!

> (He moves to strike ALF)

DOT: Stop it!

> (Pause as all three look away in embarrassment)

I'll go and wake him.

TED: Alf, you'll have to pay for this... you mark my words.

> (DOT shakes HONEY by the shoulder)

ALF: Harder!

DOT: Wait.

> (She puts a hand on his brow. HONEY stirs, finally sits up and stares about him, his eyes settling on his bag. He smiles)

ALF: Now, Mister Coffey, just you pick up that bag of yours and clear out, understand? We don't want you here.

DOT: Alf, you're not going to talk to him that way. Mr. Honey's going to stay... and I'm going to look after him.

ALF: Prostitute!

TED: Now come off it, man.

ALF: Ponce!

TED: Now you see, Dottie, why I'm.... through.

DOT: It's the drink you know, the drink. The doctor said...

            (She breaks off as HONEY stands confusedly
            by his bag.)

ALF: Now go on... pick it up and walk!

            (Dazed, HONEY seems to be trying to
            remember something)

DOT: No, Mr. Honey, you're not to touch it... to touch it.

TED: That's right, son, you leave it where it is.

ALF: Pick the blasted thing up I tell you!

DOT: No, you're to leave it alone!

ALF: Pick it up!

            (As HONEY stoops to pick up the bag TED
            comes and kicks it aside)

TED: Just you leave it where it is, son.

            (HONEY gazes from one to the other)

HONEY: Leave it?   Leave what?

TED & DOT: The bag!

ALF: (swinging on TED)   For Chris' sake, man, can't
            you see that that man's mad!

TED: No, Alf. All I see is some kind of a cripple... a
            man without kith and kin maybe... knocked about and
            bushed as I said.   The man needs bed and board, Alf,
            and it's up to us to provide it.

ALF: Why you.... you....

            (Fuming, he raises his clubbed hands and
            brings them down hard on his fat thighs.
            As he makes to repeat the action his face
            collapses and he cries out in pain as he

grabs his game leg and nurses it)

Now look... look what you've done... look what you've
gone and done to me and me a cripple... ruined and
done before me time and yet... look what you've gone
and done and me a cripple... done before me time
and yet... all I was trying to do... was trying to do
was... to stick... stick by the bloody sane and yet...

> (He drops his head and moans as TED kneels
> before him and begins to roll up his trouser
> leg)

TED: Now Alf, Alfie boy, listen... listen to me.

ALF: All I was trying to do was to... and yet, what... look
what you made me do and I a .... ruined.

TED: (beginning to massage the leg)   Alfie, remember,
remember before Jerry broke our flank in seventeen
how the Butcher... the old Butcher himself came
down our lines and told us how we'd all be dining in
Paris in a fortnight?

ALF: All I was trying to do was to stand by the sane and yet
you allowed that... that saint bloke to better me...
to get the better of me in my own house as if I was
nothing but a Hindu and yet.... there's this poor old
leg o' mine...

> (He shakes his head from side to side)

TED: All it needs is a bit of a rub, Alfie boy... a bit of a
rub, now come on, smile man, smile.

ALF: No, I'm done smiling... I'm... I'm... done.

> (He drops his head on his chest and begins
> to weep silently)

DOT: (coming and putting a hand on his shoulder) Alf....
don't.... don't, dear. It's all right now.

> (TED rises)

TED: Let him be, Dottie - he'll sleep it off now. But we'd
better get him to bed. Will you help me lift him,
Dottie?

> (She nods and together they raise ALF out
> of his chair)

There, that does it, Alfie boy - that does it, corporal.
By jove though, he's heavy all right.

(They begin to walk him to the hall door)

DOT: It's the drink.   The doctor said he mustn't, but then
you know Alf.

TED: Ay, I'm beginning to think I do.

DOT: Ted, don't worry, I'll undress him. I'll manage.

(TED opens the door)

TED: Not on your life, Dottie... you've enough to do. I'll
fix it... I'll look after Alfie boy. And Dottie... you
know I wouldn't go and leave you in a jam, don't you?
I'll stick around.   After all, who the hell is mister
Chambers anyway?

(TED and ALF go out. DOT turns slowly
and walks past HONEY who still stands by
his bag. She sits.)

DOT: You mustn't mind Mr. Lister. He doesn't mean what
he says. It's just that leg of his that makes him that
way together with what he had to put up with in the war.
So you mustn't worry... really you mustn't. It's
going to be all right. And you'll be comfortable here...
I'll see to that. And if you don't want to share then
I'll see to it later on that you get a room of your own
with a decent eiderdown and a fire. You'll like that,
won't you?

(Pause)

Well you would, I'm sure of it. There's a little room
just below the attic. Mr. Lister uses it as a kind of
store room - old souvenirs and bits of furniture but
we can find somewhere else for them. There's a
small window too that looks out over the roof tops and
on clear days you can see the hills.... and the pigeons
come.   Mr. Lister had a brother who once lived in it
... a nice quiet man who passed away some years ago.
He loved that room. He used to say to me - that room's
the best in the house, Dot. A coat of paint would make
it beautiful. It gets the sun too... and the moonlight.

(Pause as she looks up)

Have you ever thought just how like an eye the moon is?

(Pause)

No, well I suppose not. It's not really like an eye, is it? More like a globe - another world. A world that they say is.... dead.

(She rises and slowly turns to HONEY who looks at her with great compassion)

You know, I know I shouldn't talk about this but sometimes I get bothered and... worry... worry about what's going to happen here when Alf and Ted are gone and Moll gets married again and I'm left... left alone here with only Hinds and Hinds... oh hold me, please... just for a tick... till I can pull myself together.

(Slowly HONEY raises his hands which tremble. OFF MOLL is heard - faintly)

MOLL: (OFF) Dot... are you there, Dot? Dot... I've got to talk to you. Dot!

(As he stares at his trembling hands and shakes his head DOT goes to HONEY)

DOT: Oh, my dear, my poor... poor... dear.

(She cradles him in her arms)

You're safe now... safe... safe.

MOLL: (OFF - LOUDER) Dot, are you there, Dot? Are you there?

DOT: There... you're safe now... safe.

MOLL: (OFF) Dot!

(As the door handle rattles the CURTAIN FALLS)

OH DAVID, ARE YOU THERE ?

CHARACTERS

A MAN of sixty-odd

A WOMAN of the same age

A YOUTH of seventeen/eighteen

SCENE: Two armchairs facing one another: a telephone on a small
table, a door.   A male window dummy dressed in shabby evening
clothes stands off centre.   As the CURTAIN RISES the phone rings -
stops - then rings again with urgency.   As it stops a MAN of sixty-
odd enters dressed in a shabby suit.   He hangs up an overcoat on a
hatrack, then approaches the dummy.   Nods to it intimately.

MAN: You heard her now, you heard what she said to me this
          morning.   She said...Australia is a man's country, she
          said, which I instantly refuted.   I said to her...now look
          here, you common purveyor of information, what would
          you know about the Antipodes?   Why, I said, you've a
          mind like a birdcage - full of useless droppings.   But he
          died out there, she said.   Now you hold your witless
          tongue, I said, and let him live in peace.   Let him live,
          I said.

          (Phone rings)

          Don't answer it, David - let it ring.

          (It stops)

          There, you see, it's stopped.   It's her, you know.   I'd
          know that jingle anywhere.   You can't mistake it.   It's
          nervous and sanctimonious.   It's harsh.   It's full of
          insidious rigmarole.   And some day I'm going to cut
          those wires...you see if I don't...you see.

          (Sighing, he sits in one of the chairs and stares ahead.
          THE YOUTH softly enters and takes up a position by the
          dummy.   Suddenly the man strikes his thigh.)

          He was a yob, you know - a rotten little haberdasher
          posing as a Christian gentleman.   Look here I said...
          what's the flippin' game?   Who do you think you're trying
          to con, you sod?   What kind of a lousy scate do you think
          I am?
          For three pound ten I'll even wrap it up, he said.
          Now you be respectable, I said, and take those lousy
          clothes off it.
          Not on your life, he said.
          What?
          Not on your life.   You can't take a naked dummy into the
          streets.
          That's an aspersion against my character, I said.
          I can't help that, he said.   The law says that creature
          must be clothed.
          When I want the law's opinion I'll commit a felony, I said.
          You will if you take out that dummy in the buff.
          Good grief, I said, looking down at his uneducated face.
          Anyone would think the party was aroused.
          You keep it clean and sweet, he said, and smirked.

The hell you say, I said, and took you out of there.
Wrapped. Trussed up like a bloody fowl. I could have
puked.

(Mumbling to himself he swings about and sees the youth
twirling a watch on a chain.)

What...what the blazes do you want?

YOUTH: I've something to say to you.

MAN: Then I won't listen, you hear me, I won't listen.

YOUTH: Father was coming up here to set about you with the
strap but I happened to change his mind.

MAN: Why?

YOUTH: Because I want to talk to you.

MAN: You just leave me alone!

YOUTH: You're a bit of a disgrace, old son, you know that?

MAN: Now look here...

YOUTH: After all, I'll be drawing eighteen bob a week at the Public
Works and I'm only a year older than you.

MAN: Yes, but look at you...why, you're a puny...

(Fascinated, he watches the twirling watch on its chain.
Observing his interest the youth twirls it faster.)

YOUTH: It has something written on the back. Do you want to know
what it is?

MAN: I'm not interested.

(Grinning, the youth stops the watch and turns it over.)

YOUTH: It says... to Clem Mulqueen - the top of his class...
1919. The top of his class, old son, the top of the ruddy
pile.

MAN: Now you look here...

YOUTH: And what were you ever top of, Davey boy?

MAN: Myself!

YOUTH: And is that worth eighteen bob a week?

MAN: That's all very well but I happen to know things you don't.

YOUTH: Really? And what would you know what I don't? Maybe you ought to testify a bit for our mutual edification. Father might be interested.

MAN: I happen to know about life, that's what!

YOUTH: What do you mean... life?

MAN: Life's living and all the swot in the world won't stand up to it - that's for sure.

YOUTH: Yes, but considering I'll be getting eighteen bob a week at the Public Works while you get nothing is it worth it, Davey boy, is it worth it?

MAN: Damn it, I've as many brains as you have!

YOUTH: Of course you have but then - are they worth eighteen bob a week? That's the question. For eighteen bob a week's eighteen bob, isn't it? Why, you can entertain on that... take a tart out... buy a pair of silver studs.

MAN: Which end up in the hock shop - I know all about that.

YOUTH: But that's life, Davey boy, that's life.

MAN: (gesturing) You know nothing about life, understand - nothing!

YOUTH: All the same I know what life means to you.

MAN: Rubbish - you know nothing.

YOUTH: But I've seen you.

MAN: What do you mean... you've seen me?

YOUTH: I've seen you perform.

MAN: (rising) Why you rotten little tyke, I'll...

YOUTH: Now don't get nasty, Davey boy, don't get nasty. After all, we're brothers, aren't we? I mean... let's keep what we've got in the family.

MAN: What the heck are you on about?

YOUTH: I'm on about her, old son, her. Lucy. You see... I've seen you.

MAN: Seen me... where?

YOUTH: In Foxberry Wood.

MAN: So what...I was decent, wasn't I...I was decent?

YOUTH: Well you had no conscience.

MAN: So I deflowered the girl. So what? It's human nature, isn't it - a biological necessity? (He grins) Besides... it's good for the health.

YOUTH: But, Davey boy, you didn't.

MAN: You dirty liar!

YOUTH: You fumbled, man, fumbled.

MAN: Now you look here...

YOUTH: You were like a paralytic in gardening gloves.

MAN: Why you...you...

YOUTH: All thumbs and apologies.

MAN: (holding out his hands) Yet I'll have you know these hands could play the piano!

YOUTH: Yes, but you played her the wrong way, old son - the wrong way.

MAN: I'm not ashamed of that.

YOUTH: But you soiled her dress.

MAN: I what?

YOUTH: You soiled her dress and she cried.

MAN: She did?

YOUTH: She said...oh what will my mother say. (He mimics a strident female voice) Lucy, if you marry that ne'er-do-well you'll live to regret it!

MAN: (pointing to dummy) Yet he stands there unashamed!

YOUTH: All the same you had no conscience.

MAN: But I didn't need one, damn it, for I was...decent and obliging and upstanding and noble in my way and even... respectable. (Youth snickers) Now look here, you watch your step!

YOUTH: I don't only watch my steps, old son, I count 'em, and at the last analysis they led right up into the offices of the Public Works...

MAN: And to eighteen lousy bob a week and an old tin watch. Well if you want my opinion...

YOUTH: Which I don't.

MAN: Why you lousy little tick...

(Phone rings. The man picks up the receiver.)

I told you, didn't I, to leave me alone!

(He slams down the receiver.)

YOUTH: Who was it?

MAN: Her. Who else would it be?

YOUTH: Lucy?

MAN: Why, only the other day she was saying to me...

YOUTH: David, why don't we go to Australia and start afresh. It's a man's country out there...a great country...full of opportunities and little kangaroos.

MAN: Why don't you knock it off?

YOUTH: I'm past that now.

MAN: Then leave me alone.

YOUTH: But she was so romantic it was disgusting.

MAN: You don't have to tell me that.

YOUTH: Then why, old son, why?

MAN: You wouldn't understand. You see, she needed me. She was lost until I sort of resurrected her. You never saw such a mess in all your born days. If it hadn't been for me she would have failed in her purpose.

YOUTH: Her purpose?

MAN: Look here, I don't want to think about it.

YOUTH: Her purpose?

MAN: I told you to belt up.

YOUTH: Why, the only purpose she had was...

MAN: Cut that out!

YOUTH: The only purpose she had was between...

MAN: Wh-oa!

YOUTH: Have I exposed a delicate intelligence?

MAN: You've unleashed a filthy mind.

YOUTH: Then let's change the subject.

MAN: We've nothing to talk about.

YOUTH: What about that eighteen bob a week?

MAN: I don't want to know about that, for I was slaving my guts out trying to... trying to decide what to do with my life while you were gallivanting about trying to ruin my reputation.

YOUTH: But you got me wrong, Davey boy. I was trying to build you up.

MAN: To build me up?

YOUTH: Of course. I was investing in good will.

MAN: By aiding and abetting vicious propaganda?

YOUTH: No, old son. All I did...

MAN: Was to distort my reputation. But the point is, boy, you failed - as they all failed - as that bitch of a mother failed. Christ, I can hear her now. (He mimics strident female voice) Lucy, if you marry that ne'er-do-well you'll live to regret it. I tell you, I ought to have (gestures) defected after what she did to me!

YOUTH: You mean... she ruined your reputation?

MAN: Who cares a damn about that now when... when...

BOTH: (pointing at dummy)   He stands there unashamed!

(Pause as man stares at the grinning youth. As he slowly raises his hand to make a blow the phone rings. As he impatiently turns to lift the receiver the youth quietly exits.)

MAN: (on phone) I told you to leave me alone!

(Slamming down the receiver he glances about him.
Confused, he stands subdued before the dummy and puts
his hands on its shoulders.)

The point is, David my son, they think you were defeated.

(Lights down)

(Lights up: MAN sits in chair staring ahead as the door
springs open to admit a WOMAN of sixty-odd dragging
a large brown-paper parcel. Humming to herself, she
unwraps it and displays a large, new Electrolux.)

WOMAN: (stepping back) There...what a beauty! I love it. And
if David hadn't died in Australia he would have loved it
too.

MAN: I love, she loves, we loved, they looked on. Now
there's jurisprudence.

WOMAN: Australia is a man's country, he said, which I instantly
refuted. I said to him...now what would you know about
the Antipodes? Why, I said, you have a mind like a
birdcage.

MAN: There's nothing wrong with him, I tell you, nothing
wrong.

WOMAN: Then why did he go to Australia?

MAN: Because he had a chance out there...a chance.

WOMAN: To do what?

MAN: To rise to the top, that's what!

WOMAN: But he died out there.

MAN: Will you kindly leave him alone!

WOMAN: (gazing at the ceiling) David dear, can you hear me?

MAN: I said will you leave him alone!

WOMAN: Stop shouting. You'll ruin the contact.

MAN: For Chris' sake...

(He begins to rise when phone rings and he is frozen into
immobility.)

MAN: Don't...don't answer it.

WOMAN: You don't understand...it's there to be answered.

          (She reaches for the receiver.)

MAN: (shouts) I said don't answer it!

WOMAN: But I have to...it might be David.

MAN: (pointing at dummy) But he stands there unashamed!

WOMAN: (picking up receiver) Shush. Hullo...hullo...Oh David
          dear, I knew you'd call.

          (Man groans and shrinks into his chair.)

          Now tell me, is God well?

          (Man groans.)

          You don't say... now who would have believed it?
          You say he caught a cold? Well, he must be more
          careful. What, dear? No, dear. I can't get away just
          yet for you know how it is. I mean to say he's so
          terribly down if you know what I mean. So terribly down.

MAN: He's all right I tell you - on the flaming up and up.

WOMAN: Oh David dear, I wish they'd take him away, I really do.

MAN: He's got the makings of a King, I tell you, a King!

WOMAN: Of course, dear - you had better put her on.

MAN: A King! A glorious, unmitigated King - an unadulterated
          one!

WOMAN: Oh thank you, thank you, your Ladyship - you're so very
          kind.

          (Slowly she lowers the receiver.)

MAN: I tell you it's disgusting.

WOMAN: That...was God's mother.

MAN: Will you listen to me!

WOMAN: There's fever in heaven. David was hoarse.

MAN: David was never hoarse - he had a voice like a trumpet.
          You should have heard his echo!

WOMAN: But he was never out of flannel vests.

MAN: Why, he could fight, that boy...he could fight like the dickens. I remember the fight he had with...with... Charlie Dickens...Charlie Harrison it was...Charlie ...what's-his-name.

WOMAN: He used to cry himself to sleep in my arms.

MAN: He hated sex - I know that.

WOMAN: He hated everything.

MAN: Yet he stands there unashamed!

WOMAN: God's mother told me he was doomed from the start.

MAN: He was a rebel - that's what he was. A beautiful, well set-up rebel. Why, look at him!

(He points at dummy.)

WOMAN: Now where did I put my knitting?

(She looks about her.)

MAN: A rebel - and would still have been but for circumstances.

WOMAN: Now where's that...ah!

(She finds knitting beneath a chair cushion.)

MAN: Given his fair share of luck he would have licked the world.

WOMAN: (shaking her head) The way he used to cough in his hand... it was dreadful.

MAN: Yet he stands there...(begins to cough)

WOMAN: He didn't have the gumption for shame for he was a failure from the very beginning. I well remember mother saying (mimicking strident female voice) Lucy, if you marry that ne'er-do-well you'll live to regret it!

(Pause)

MAN: She's dead, thank God.

WOMAN: Yes, but if he hadn't gone to Australia we might have saved him.

MAN: That was a man's country but he had to drag a woman along...the idiot.

108

WOMAN: Just let him be, for God's mother's sake!

MAN: (rising and approaching dummy) Let him be, you say!
Damn it, I swear if you let him be he'll ruin us...he'll
bring down dirt on our name...that's what he'll do...
and distort our reputation by aiding and abetting a
vicious propaganda!

WOMAN: But he's quite a help sometimes.

MAN: Well I haven't seen him display any fortitude - he's
failed at everything.

WOMAN: He couldn't help it for his defeats were foreordained.

MAN: That's right - bugger the works over his bleeding
waterloos.

WOMAN: That happens to be a privilege I won't give up.

MAN: Please yourself but I'm going to have a chat with that
article and if he doesn't bend his ear a bit I'm going to
(to dummy) strap the flaming hide off you, you hear that?

(Pause)

Now where's my strap?

WOMAN: I won't stand for anything like that now. I'm too tired...
too worn out...and we owe three pound ten for electric
light. It's disgraceful.

MAN: Now, you keep your hair on for I'm prepared to do
something about them bills though I can't help thinking
that if everyone pulled their weight in this house this kind
of thing wouldn't happen. Fact is if David, now, was
working his eighteen bob a week would be a very useful
sum indeed. Very useful.

WOMAN: At his age I was out working my fingers to the bone. Now
where's that strap?

MAN: It's in the scullery behind the door. But why not let me
have a talk with him?

WOMAN: What good can it do?

MAN: Well you know how it is...how he used to listen to me
tell him what was righteous and half decent in this world.
How he could improve himself if only he'd pull himself
together and get on with it - straighten himself out -turn
over a new leaf - pick himself up - get a move on - come
to his senses - marshall his forces and stop blotting his

MAN: bloody copybook!   (to dummy)   You hear that!
(Cont.)

WOMAN: That's all very well but I don't see what you can do what
          I can't.   All that young man needs is a good thrashing.

MAN: But then brute force is not my way, is it?   I don't mean
          to say that a good thrashing wouldn't do him good, but
          seeing he won't talk to you it's just possible he might
          talk to me - mightn't he?

WOMAN: I wish he would for Our Lord said that as the child was
          very often father to the man...

MAN: Don't be ridiculous.

WOMAN: If you're going to be insulting I shall go to my room -
          immediately.

          (She begins to gather her knitting.)

MAN: Now wait a moment.

WOMAN: The holy word will not bear scoffing at.   Good-bye,
          good night, good riddance.

          (She doesn't move.   Man scowls and nods his head.)

MAN: I see.

WOMAN: See what?

MAN: You don't trust me, do you?

WOMAN: Why?

MAN: Because left alone with him I might have done him harm.

WOMAN: What?

MAN: I don't know but some harm or other - believe me.

WOMAN: How?

MAN: Being angry, I would have sneaked up on him probably and
          cold-cocked him from behind.   (He chuckles and gestures
          with his fists.)

WOMAN: Well I won't stand for anything like that.

MAN: What do you mean...you won't stand for it?

WOMAN: It's disgusting, primitive, incorrigible, and insane.

MAN: Then what insurrection would you have me do?

WOMAN: Talk to him like I said.

MAN: But what'll I say?

WOMAN: Anything - so long as it's the truth.

MAN: Yes, but is it any use?

WOMAN: You can only try.

MAN: But will he listen?

WOMAN: Of course he will if you tell him the holy word won't bear
          scoffing at.

MAN: All right, I'll try.

          (He faces dummy and clears his throat.)

          Now you listen here, boxer boy, what's the flippin' game,
          eh? Just who do you think you're trying to con, you sod.
          Just what kind of a lousy skate do you think I am, eh?
          Why, I ought to knock that Judas grin right off your flaming
          nelly...

WOMAN: Stop it!

MAN: And ruin the contact?

WOMAN: That's not the way to talk to him.

MAN: What's wrong with it?

WOMAN: It's raucous, that's what it is. Plead with him a bit.

MAN: Plead?

WOMAN: That's right. Be soft and paternal. Be refined.

MAN: (after pause) How?

WOMAN: Kid him a bit. Tell him that he's the apple of our eye.

MAN: You mean...lower the tone a bit?

WOMAN: You don't have to do that - just lower your voice a bit.

MAN: (softly) Like that?

WOMAN: That's better - he'll listen now.

MAN: (clearing throat and facing dummy) Now you hear what she said, Davey boy, so I do therefore request that you put this hypothecation into effect as of June ninth, 1919, and provide your godly parents with an acknowledgment that the hypothecation shall go into effect as of that date together with Schedule A to conform with present security holdings - namely, that you wake up to yourself and put the bit between your teeth for you've a great future, son, (louder) a great future. Why, you could soar to the top, me boy, and who knows - be like your brother Clem who's earning eighteen bloody bob a week (louder) while you, you filthy lay-about...

WOMAN: You're shouting!

MAN: I can't help that - he provokes me.

WOMAN: Then take the strap to him.

MAN: No. I'll talk to him like I said.

WOMAN: But he won't listen.

MAN: Then I'll expose him to ridicule!

WOMAN: But he won't listen!

MAN: Then I'll set him an example!

WOMAN: But he'll provoke you!

MAN: Then I'll...I'll...

WOMAN: Get rid of him!

MAN: But he won't listen!

WOMAN: Then I'll ring God's mother.

MAN: I wish you wouldn't.

WOMAN: She'll know what to do.

MAN: But I could speak to him.

WOMAN: But he stands there unashamed!

MAN: It's the times I tell you - they're much too soft.

WOMAN: Then talk to him.

MAN: But what'll I say?

WOMAN: Tell him the truth about himself.

MAN: But he's so lonely it's hard to get a word across.

WOMAN: That's because he's self-satisfied.

MAN: Yet I've seen him desperate before today - desperate.
Why, you should have seen him the day he fought Charlie..
Charlie Buonorotti, I think it was. By God he was
rebellious!

WOMAN: Did he ever bring home the bacon?

MAN: Never mind about that - he grew up proud!

WOMAN: Then what happened to him?

MAN: (quietly) He went to Australia.

WOMAN: Why?

MAN: Because it was a man's country.

WOMAN: Then why did he fail?

MAN: He took a woman along.

WOMAN: And soiled her dress?

MAN: He didn't, I tell you, he didn't. (Triumphantly) He...
deflowered her!

WOMAN: (Sitting with her head in her hands) It was awful.

MAN: Yet his dreams, you know, were beautiful. (He gestures)
All the poetry in the world was gathered in his head
while his hands, you know, his hands... could play the
piano.

(Music off.)

(The YOUTH enters softly and stands by the dummy,
quietly twirling his watch.)

And there wasn't a thing he couldn't play... even by ear:
Beethoven, Schubert... little Annie Laurie. On clear,
crystal nights when the air was still his little brother
Clem would come and whistle by his side.

(Youth softly whistles "Danny Deever". Man's face
lights up.)

MAN:
(Cont.)
And all the family would be standing there - their eyes aglow like fireflies - their hearts beating like the wings of trembling birds...

(As Youth raspberries, man wheels and clutches at a knitting needle on the table.)

That's done it!

YOUTH: Easy, Davey boy, easy.

MAN: (Obsessed by the twirling watch) What...what are you doing here?

YOUTH: To check on Lucy - that's all.

MAN: You just leave her alone, you hear me, just leave her alone!

YOUTH: What's wrong, old son - jealous?

MAN: I'm proud, that's what.

YOUTH: Proud that you soiled her dress?

MAN: Now you look here...

YOUTH: Proud that you ballsed it up?

MAN: Why you rotten little postage clerk, I'll show you...

YOUTH: Show me what? That you're a better man than I am, Gunga Din?

MAN: Damn it - I did all right.

YOUTH: Where...in Australia?

(Man nods.)

Then why did you come back?

MAN: They hated his red cheeks - that's why.

YOUTH: Go on.

MAN: There's nothing more to say.

YOUTH: But I want to know about his cheeks - his red ones.

MAN: There's nothing more to tell. They were his stigmata.

YOUTH: You mean ... like Cain?

MAN: No, like Esau. For he was a tough, hairy little fellow with ideas as sweet as holy smoke only no one would listen to him, no one cared, for he was a flower, that boy, with sharp and dreadful petals...his centre crimson.. all shot with little lights...

(Youth smirks)

...only you pissed on his good name and ruined his reputation!

(He brandishes the knitting needle.)

YOUTH: Don't!

(Puzzled yet fascinated, man lowers his hand as he takes in the twirling watch. He totters forward to take a better look at it.)

Do you want to know what's written on the back?

(Man nods. Youth turns the watch over.)

See...it says...to David - with love. Lucy. See?

(He points to inscription as man bends over it.)

MAN: You mean to tell me that...that watch is mine?

YOUTH: That's right.

MAN: That I earned it?

YOUTH: Of course.

MAN: That it was given to me?

YOUTH: Who else?

MAN: That there's no two ways about it?

YOUTH: Absolutely.

MAN: (menacingly) Then what's it doing on your chain?

YOUTH: I knocked it off.

MAN: You what?

YOUTH: I nicked it.

MAN: Where?

YOUTH: In the bushes.

MAN: In the bushes?

YOUTH: Boy, you should have seen him.

MAN: You mean...he was pretty good?

YOUTH: Of course he was. I mean he could be kind and apologetic, couldn't he? He could even be undignified.

MAN: Now wait a moment.

YOUTH: Undignified. You know...humble...contrite... compassionate...sincere and insurmountable. In other words - a veritable little ball of fire, his centre crimson, all shot with little lights...

MAN: Now stop it, stop it now, stop it!

YOUTH: And he didn't mind, did he, the lack of understanding and the disgrace of not being able to touch a penny of that eighteen bob a week?

MAN: He was done out of it, that's why.

YOUTH: I know.

MAN: It was nicked like that watch of his.

YOUTH: (proffering the watch) You want it?

(Man makes a grab for it: Youth whisks it away.)

MAN: Now wait a tick...

YOUTH: Try again.

(Man makes a grab for it: Youth whisks it away.)

See, you're slow, old son. Slow and undignified.

MAN: I was off balance, that's all. Now...now...come on and hand me over what's rightfully mine...what's my birthright.

YOUTH: You want that eighteen bob a week as well?

MAN: I want what's mine, what I earned, what I sweated for!

(He reaches out a hand: it trembles.)

YOUTH: Was that the hand that set the world on fire or was it the one that could only play the piano?

MAN: (clenching fist) It was the hand I tell you that sent Charlie... Charlie Dickens to the gutter!

YOUTH: The same hand that ruined poor Lucy?

MAN: Now listen here...

YOUTH: That ruined her dress?

MAN: Now cut that out!

YOUTH: If you don't believe me - ask her.

(Man swings about and blinks. Swings back from the woman to the dummy and back again. The youth stands by now, paring his nails with a knife. Confused, man scratches himself.)

Well?

MAN: She's... she's... engaged.

YOUTH: Then interrupt her.

MAN: You mean... butt in and ask her why she's ... sad?

YOUTH: That's right.

MAN: But what'll I say?

YOUTH: Ask her what the trouble is.

MAN: But she won't listen.

YOUTH: Then take the strap to her.

MAN: But brute force is not my way, is it? I mean... brute force is not my way.

YOUTH: Look, do you want me to ask her?

MAN: No... no... you'd only balls it up. I'll ask her myself.

YOUTH: Then go ahead.

MAN: All right, but then don't goad me.

(Bracing himself, he clears his throat and approaches woman.)

MAN: Now look here, you filthy whore of Babylon...what...
(Cont.)   what's the flippin' game? Just who do you think you're
          trying to con, you sod? Just what kind of a lousy skate
          do you think I am, eh?

          (Youth sniggers)

          That's right...balls it up, why don't you, balls it up!

YOUTH: But that's not the way to talk to her.

MAN: Why not?

YOUTH: It's raucous - that's what it is. Plead with her a bit.

MAN: Plead?

YOUTH: That's right. Tell her she's the apple of your eye.

MAN: Look here, I've never pleaded with anyone in my life.

YOUTH: Then do it now before it's too late.

MAN: How do you mean?

YOUTH: Like I used to.

MAN: You!

YOUTH: Of course. I used to take her in my arms and plead with
          her when you weren't there...in the bushes. Only it was
          easy, see, easy - on account of that eighteen bob a week.

MAN: You mean to tell me she went with you...my own flesh
          and blood...my own...

YOUTH: But she couldn't help it, see? She was attracted.

MAN: She was attracted to me...she said so. She was sold on
          me.

YOUTH: But then she couldn't resist me, see, because I didn't
          soil her dress.

MAN: Are you trying to tell me that you seduced her?

YOUTH: There was no need to for Barkis was willin', old son,
          Barkis was willin'.

MAN: Why, you rotten little tyke ...

          (As he moves with the needle raised the youth swings the
          watch on the chain. Man stops as if mesmerised.)

MAN: (Cont.) What...what are you doing with my watch?

YOUTH: Winding it up.

MAN: You got no right...give it to me.

(As he puts out a shaking hand the youth swings the watch through his fingers and as man clutches at it he misses it.)

Damn!

YOUTH: You've got to be quicker than that, old son, for time don't stand still, you know. Now what about Lucy?

MAN: Well, what about her?

YOUTH: Aren't you going to address her?

MAN: What the hell for?

YOUTH: To get on better terms so you can tell her how to pick herself up - get a move on - turn over a new leaf - straighten herself out - pick up the pieces and marshall her forces in order to put the bit between her teeth.

MAN: She conned me, you know. Conned me into committing myself.

YOUTH: How?

MAN: Being a religious sort of person she said to me...we're fated, that's what we are - our union was foreordained. There's nothing for it but to love each other till we die.

YOUTH: You were conned all right.

MAN: Of course I was but then what could I have done?

YOUTH: Got rid of her.

MAN: How?

YOUTH: Like I did. I gave her away.

MAN: You what?

YOUTH: I sent her back to you.

MAN: But she came to me willingly for she was in love with me... she said so.

YOUTH: You sure of that?

MAN: Of course I am. Why, she used to cry herself to sleep in my arms.

YOUTH: She hated sex, I know that.

MAN: Oh no she didn't. She used to say...

YOUTH: (in strident female voice) Mother, if I marry that ne'er-do-well I'll live to regret it!

MAN: Damn it, that's an aspersion against my character!

YOUTH: (gazing at ceiling) David dear, can you hear me?

MAN: Cut it!

YOUTH: (producing knife) With this?

MAN: What... what are you going to do with it?

YOUTH: Maybe I'll give it back to David.

MAN: Do you mean to tell me that ... that knife is his?

YOUTH: That's right - same as Lucy and the watch and that eighteen bob a week.

MAN: Then I ought to...

YOUTH: What?

MAN: Take back what's mine.

YOUTH: (juggling knife) Why don't you?

(As man lurches forward with the needle raised the youth moves and drives the blade into the heart of the dummy. As man cries out and clutches at his chest the youth grins and, backing, slowly exits.)

WOMAN: (glancing up) For God's mother's sake, what's wrong with you?

MAN: (holding his heart) I've got a pain... right here.

WOMAN: You're short of adrenalin, that's all.

MAN: But that's the second time in a month. It cuts, you know.

WOMAN: It's merely a state of being.

120

MAN: But I keep...imagining things.

WOMAN: Then deny them...deny your enemies.

MAN: How?

WOMAN: By putting some kind of a hypothecation into effect.

MAN: Of course.

WOMAN: Then rest yourself.

MAN: I can't. I worry about it.

WOMAN: It's just a question of putting matter over mind.

MAN: Yes but...

         (Phone rings.)

         Now keep away from that phone!

WOMAN: I can't...it might be David.

MAN: Don't answer it I tell you!

WOMAN: But I must!

MAN: (menacingly) I said, keep away from it.

WOMAN: But don't you see - it might be God's mother.

MAN: (shocked) Then...then...ask her how we are.

WOMAN: (taking up phone) Hullo...hullo...is anyone there?
         I said, is anyone there?

MAN: Maybe no one's there?

WOMAN: But it rang.

MAN: Perhaps it was a mistake?

WOMAN: Mistakes are not made in heaven.

MAN: Then...then...tell me why we are?

WOMAN: Shush...someone's there.

MAN: Then tell them to leave me alone.

WOMAN: Hullo...hullo...who is it, please? No, I can't hear -
         would you mind speaking up? I said, would you mind...

WOMAN: look here, there's no need to shout, is there? I said
(Cont.)   there's no need...oh, I see. Thank goodness for that...
   you're such a dear.

MAN: Who is it...God's mother?

WOMAN: No, it's David. He wants to apologise.

MAN: (pointing to dummy) What do you mean he wants to
   apologise! He never did anything wrong, did he? He
   was always above board, wasn't he? What do you mean...
   he wants to apologise?

WOMAN: He wants to apologise for having been defeated.

MAN: Defeated my right hand tit! That boy might have been a
   bit of a failure but he was never defeated, you hear me,
   never! Not even in the depression was he defeated or
   during the war. Not even after the war. Not even on
   his honeymoon! He was jeopardized, that's all. Got at.
   Besmirched and underrated. He knew too much.

WOMAN: Then why does he want to apologise?

MAN: It's wicked what they say for that boy had brains and
   guile and pluck. Why, he even knew how to...deny his
   enemies.

WOMAN: (into phone) David dear, I hope you'll forgive the
   hypothecation but you know how it is - he gets so jealous.

MAN: He hated sex, that's all.

WOMAN: What, love? Oh, just the same old thing - knitting a bit,
   you know. No dear, I can't hear...you sound so hoarse.

MAN: He was strong, that boy - as strong as an ox. Ask
   Charlie...Charlie...what's-his-name.

WOMAN: No dear, no one said anything. You will! Oh glory be -
   how wonderful!

MAN: Don't listen to them, my son, don't listen.

WOMAN: But that's what I always said, didn't I? Wait and the
   world waits with you, fly and you fly alone.

   (She giggles: Man groans.)

   Oh, just the same, you know. (She studies dummy.)
   A little envious and despondent and so terribly, terribly
   hurt.

MAN: (holding his heart)   Just a bit short of adrenalin and matter over mind.

WOMAN: Still, that's the way of the world, isn't it - one goes up while the other goes down.

MAN: That's a lie!

WOMAN: Oh mostly down, dear, most terribly terribly down.

MAN: He rode high, I tell you!

WOMAN: Of course I will, my love...I'll tell the world.

MAN: That's what's called aiding and abetting a vicious propaganda.

WOMAN: And thank her ladyship for me, won't you...that's a dear. And David...

MAN: The point is...I'm tired. (He sits)

WOMAN: Remember I love you, dear...I love you.

(As she blows kisses into the mouthpiece, Man grimaces and sinks deeper into his chair.)

(putting phone down)   That was David.

MAN: How can he be in two places at once?

WOMAN: He rang to say that he'd got his wings.

MAN: (startled) His what?

WOMAN: His wings.

MAN: Do you mean to stand there and tell me...

WOMAN: Yes. He's a member now of the hierarchy.

MAN: A success, is he?

WOMAN: Well - he's getting established.

MAN: Pulling rank, is he?

WOMAN: Well - he's been spoken for.

MAN: By God's mother?

WOMAN: No. Her son.

MAN: Her what?

WOMAN: Her only begotten.

MAN: So it's over, is it?

WOMAN: Well, there's no need to speak to him now.

MAN: No.

WOMAN: And you can burn that strap.

MAN: Yes.

WOMAN: I'm so glad he died in Australia now, aren't you?

MAN: I dare say he tried to hang on.

WOMAN: But he surrendered so easily.

MAN: I dare say he had no choice.

WOMAN: But he was always so defeated.

MAN: Then he must have been lonely.

WOMAN: But he was married.

MAN: Then he must have been desperate.

WOMAN: But he hated everything.

MAN: Then he must have been...He got his wings, you say?

WOMAN: Sinners and failures always get them.

MAN: You don't say?

WOMAN: For the weak and the defeated shall inherit the pastures of heaven.

MAN: That's something.

WOMAN: And glory ever after shall brighten their names.

MAN: Are you sure of that - are you sure?

WOMAN: Of course.

MAN: Then I'm tired...I'm very tired.

WOMAN: Now I wonder where my knitting is?

MAN: In Australia.

        (Leaning back he closes his eyes. Phone rings. His arms hang loose and he stares at the ceiling as the woman picks up the phone.)

WOMAN: Oh David dear, is that you? I said, is that you, dear? What? Look dear, can you hear me? I said...can-you-hear-me? No. I mean...can-you-hear...

        (She shakes phone.)

        I'm sure it rang, aren't you?

        (As she sees man she drops the receiver and leaves it swinging on its hook. The stage darkens. Slowly she reaches out and tugs man's sleeve.)

        David dear...David love...Can you hear me, dear?

        (Pause)

        David, I said...David...Oh David, are you there?

CURTAIN